BLACK & DECKER®

THE COMPLETE GUIDE TO
ROOFING & SIDING

Install • Finish • Repair • Maintain

CREATIVE
PUBLISHING
international

CHANHASSEN, MINNESOTA

www.creativepub.com

Contents

Copyright © 2004
Creative Publishing international, Inc.
18705 Lake Drive East
Chanhassen, Minnesota 55317
1-800-328-3895
www.creativepub.com
All rights reserved

Printed on American Paper by: Quebecor World

10 9 8 7 6 5 4 3 2 1

President/CEO: Michael Eleftheriou
Vice President/Publisher: Linda Ball
Vice President/Retail Sales & Marketing: Kevin Haas

Executive Editor: Bryan Trandem
Creative Director: Tim Himsel
Managing Editor: Michelle Skudlarek
Editorial Director: Jerri Farris

Lead Editor: Brett Martin
Copy Editor: Barbara Harold
Proofreader: Janice Cauley
Senior Art Director: Dave Schelitzche
Mac Designer: Jon Simpson
Technical Illustrators: Dave Schelitzche, Jon Simpson
Technical Photo Editor: Randy Austin
Project Manager: Tracy Stanley
Photo Researcher: Jeanette Moss McCurdy
Studio Services Manager: Jeanette Moss McCurdy
Photographer: Tate Carlson, Andrea Rugg
Scene Shop Carpenter: Glenn Austin, Randy Austin,
  Marcus Landrum
Director of Production Services and Photography: Kim Gerber
Production Manager: Helga Thielen

THE COMPLETE GUIDE TO ROOFING & SIDING
Created by: The Editors of Creative Publishing international, Inc.,
in cooperation with Black & Decker. Black & Decker is a trademark
of The Black & Decker Corporation and is used under license.

Library of Congress
Cataloging-in-Publication Data
on file

   ISBN 1-58923-154-6 (soft cover)

Portions of The Complete Guide to Roofing & Siding are taken from the Black & Decker® books Carpentry: Remodeling, Exterior Home Repairs & Improvements, Home Masonry Projects & Repairs. Other titles from Creative Publishing international include:

The New Everyday Home Repairs; Basic Wiring & Electrical Repairs; Building Decks; Home Masonry Projects & Repairs; Workshop Tips & Techniques; Home Plumbing Projects & Repairs; Advanced Home Wiring; Advanced Deck Building; Bathroom Remodeling; Built-In Projects for the Home; Landscape Design & Construction; Refinishing & Finishing Wood; Building Porches & Patios; Flooring Projects & Techniques; Advanced Home Plumbing; Remodeling Kitchens; Finishing Basements & Attics; Stonework & Masonry Projects; Sheds, Gazebos & Outbuildings; Building & Finishing Walls & Ceilings; The Complete Guide to Home Plumbing; The Complete Guide to Home Wiring;

The Complete Guide to Building Decks; The Complete Guide to Painting & Decorating; The Complete Guide to Creative Landscapes; The Complete Guide to Home Masonry; The Complete Guide to Home Carpentry; The Complete Guide to Home Storage; The Complete Guide to Bathrooms; The Complete Guide to Easy Woodworking Projects; The Complete Guide to Flooring; The Complete Guide to Ceramic & Stone Tile; The Complete Guide to Kitchens; The Complete Photo Guide to Home Repair; The Complete Photo Guide to Home Improvement; The Complete Photo Guide to Outdoor Home Improvement.

Introduction

Nothing plays a greater role in the look and protection of your home than roofing and siding. They're the most visible elements of your home, and they're the first things people notice when they visit or pass by your house. They're also your main defenses against rain, snow, wind, and inclement weather.

Roofing and siding set the character, color scheme, and tone for your home. Faded, bleak walls will come alive by replacing the worn out siding with beautiful new wood, attractive vinyl, rustic log cabin, or durable masonry siding. A dull, uninteresting roof will get new life when the stale shingles are replaced with a vibrant metal, three-dimensional or colored asphalt, attractive wood shakes, or distinctive clay roofing.

Replacing your own roofing and siding can be

very rewarding. You'll see the results of your hard work every day, as will all of your guests and visitors. By doing the work yourself, you'll also save a bundle of money—up to 50 percent of the cost of some roofing and siding projects is labor.

The Complete Guide to Roofing & Siding is the first comprehensive book to walk homeowners through every aspect of roofing and siding projects—from choosing the right materials, to planning the project, to detailed installation steps, to maintaining your exterior for years to come. In addition to roofing and siding, this book covers other exterior projects, including painting, installing soffits and fascia, hanging gutters, and putting in ventilation systems.

The book opens with a Portfolio of Roofing & Siding that features the very latest products

available for your exterior. You'll find innovative designs and popular styles that will help you choose products that are right for your home.

Planning for New Roofing & Siding, the second section, will help you prepare for your project. You'll learn how to evaluate your needs, order materials, prepare the job site, and work safely.

The following two sections, Roofing Installation and Siding Installation, are the heart of the book. These sections cover the installation processes for the best roofing and siding products on the market. The step-by-step instructions and color photographs show professional installation techniques for all of the popular roofing and siding products, including asphalt shingles, metal roofing, cedar shakes and shingles, tile roofing, roll roofing, vinyl siding, fiber cement, wood siding, and

log cabin siding. Other projects include finishing your walls with cement, veneer stone, or stucco.

To round out the installation processes, the next section provides detailed instructions for installing systems for soffits and fascia, gutters, and ventilation. These systems contribute to the health and well-being of your home environment.

Since painting is another way to improve your home's appearance, a section dedicated to exterior painting details how to identify paint problems, how to prepare for a paint job, and how to apply paint. Included in these instructions is information on using brushes, rollers, and airless sprayers.

The final section of the book contains everything you need to know about making exterior repairs. Most roofing and siding lasts for decades, and chances are that you'll need to make repairs at some point in time. Keep this book in a convenient location as a reference in case emergency repairs are necessary.

NOTE: The projects in this book are based on products and materials that are standard sizes in the United States. If you're using this book outside of the U.S., and the materials are based on the metric system, you may need to slightly adjust the measurements for your project.

Photo courtesy of Alside

Portfolio of Roofing & Siding

An impressive exterior is a combination of beautiful siding, attractive roofing, and complementary trim. Well-chosen exterior products will work together to enhance the look and appeal of your home, and keep the house watertight. The "perfect" siding gives the home its personality. For example, brick siding looks imposing and robust, while vinyl siding offers a contemporary look and feel.

Roofing also affects the character of a home.

Monotone asphalt shingles, for example, make a house less imposing, while a colorful metal roof can become a major decorative feature.

The inspiring photos in this section feature a wide range of roofing and siding types, styles, and materials. They're sure to generate new ideas and help you make practical decisions when choosing roofing and siding.

The deep color of the siding (above) contrasts nicely with the crisp white trim. For further contrast, the horizontal lines created by the siding are juxtaposed with the vertical lines of the board and batten siding on the gables.

Different siding materials are used to draw attention to individual sections of this house (left). Similar colors allow the sidings to complement each other in contributing to the overall design.

Elegant trim can make a bold statement on the exterior (right). This trim features fluted corners and decorative pieces above the windows and under the soffits.

Wood & Fiber Cement

Wood siding is a natural choice for homeowners who appreciate the look and texture of real wood. Wood lap siding is a typical siding for homes across the country (left).

Log cabin siding brings old-time charm to modern housing. It's a distinctive siding product, offering a look all its own (right).

Fiber cement siding closely resembles wood. It's available in various styles, including shingles (below).

Vinyl Siding

Combining siding styles creates unique effects. The house to the left combines traditional vinyl siding with vinyl scallops and vinyl shakes. The house to the right also combines vinyl siding and vinyl shakes, separated by a broad band of vinyl trim.

A single siding style is used throughout the exterior on the house below to create a simple but elegant look. Accents are added with the shutters and trim.

Brick & Stucco

Stucco siding is often used on higher-end homes to create a majestic appearance. Stucco siding looks smooth from a distance, but up close, the textured surface is apparent (left).

Brick siding has been used for centuries to give homes a luxurious exterior (right).

Stucco siding is brought to life with trim that's painted a contrasting color (below).

Asphalt Shingles

Architectural shingles, also called dimensional shingles, offer a rugged, staggered appearance (right). The shingles are not flush along the bottom edges, so the pattern appears to be random. The roofing looks more like wood shakes than traditional asphalt shingles.

Three-tab asphalt shingles have been the standard roofing material for decades (below). The tabs align in alternate rows to give the roof a uniform appearance. The shingles are available in a multitude of colors to complement any siding.

Photo courtesy of GAF Materials Corporation; Photo (left) courtesy of CertainTeed Corporation

Photo courtesy of Metalworks; Photo (below) courtesy of Metal Sales Mfg. Corp.

Metal Roofs

A steel metal roof can mimic the look of natural slate (left). The color and style work well with this home's overall color scheme.

Copper roofs provide a remarkable touch of sophistication to a house (right). Such a unique roof draws attention, and can even become a conversation piece.

Vertical metal roofs are a good choice for rustic and log cabin homes (below). Roof panels add color, and the vertical lines create interest by contrasting with the horizontal lines of the siding.

Photo courtesy of Vulcan Metal Works, LLC.

Photo used with permission of Owens Corning

Planning for New Roofing & Siding

Careful planning is paramount for a successful roofing or siding job. It ensures that you'll be prepared for any problems that arise, will stay within your budget, and accurately estimate the amount of time and materials you'll need to complete your project. It also ensures that you'll end up with a roof and siding that meet your needs.

Thorough planning and experimenting with color combinations help guarantee that your finished roof and siding will work well together without creating undesired contrasts or color clashes. Keep in mind that styles and trends come and go quickly, but your roof and siding will last for decades. Some exterior colors and combinations never go out of fashion, but if you choose a bold color or a chic design, your exterior could look outdated in a few years.

Begin the planning process by looking at different products and materials. New roofing and siding products are continually hitting the market, and you may end up liking a product that you didn't know existed. This planning stage also allows you to weigh the advantages and disadvantages of each product. As your planning evolves, you can narrow your focus to selecting a product, color scheme, and accessories.

During your planning, make a list of the tools and materials you'll need to complete the job. Make sure you have everything needed for the project before starting, especially when specialty tools are required.

A new exterior turned this nondescript house (inset) into a colorful, inviting home (above). Nearly every component of the exterior was changed, including the roofing, fascia, soffits, siding, trim, and shutters.

Getting Started

When planning your project, consider everything that you want to change. Is it just the siding? Just the roofing? Or is it the siding, soffits, and fascia? Or the roofing and the gutters? If you want to make several changes, such as all new siding, soffits, fascia, gutters, and shutters, do them as part of a single project. This allows you to choose complementary colors, styles, and materials for everything being replaced. For roofing, determine if all or some of your flashing needs to be replaced, and make that part of the shingle replacement.

Before jumping right into the project and tearing off the old materials, plan the entire work process. Establish a logical work sequence that allows you to work efficiently without leaving your house

exposed to the elements for long periods of time. In most cases, you'll want to work on small sections of the house at a time, tearing off only as much old material as you can replace in one day. It's not a good practice to completely tear off the old roofing or siding if it will take you a couple of weeks to install the new materials.

You'll also want to install the new materials in a sequence that makes the most sense. If you're replacing the siding and the soffits, install the soffits first since the siding ends at the soffits. For roofing, install the roofing materials before installing new gutters. Think through how each component will overlap or butt against another part of the exterior. This planning will simplify the installation process and ensure a great-looking finish.

This Victorian house transcends time with its new exterior. The old roofing, siding, and trim (inset) were all replaced with modern materials (above) while preserving the home's historical elegance.

21

Your roofing and siding should meet the two fundamental needs of making your home look attractive and protecting it from the elements.

Evaluating Your Needs

There are many good reasons to replace roofing or siding—it may be leaking, reaching the end of its life span, or look sorely out of date. These reasons will probably change as your roofing and siding age. Or, you may just decide one day that your home needs a facelift, and you want to replace the roofing or siding with something more lively.

Before jumping right into a replacement project, ensure that your new roofing or siding will meet all of your objectives. If you like the look and style of your shingles but they're getting old, it's a simple matter to replace them with a newer version. On the other hand, if you're tired of maintaining your siding, you'll want a product that looks nice but doesn't require constant attention.

Also consider your future needs. If you're replacing your siding now and will need to replace your roofing in a few years, plan now for a siding that will complement the new roof. If you're installing a new soffit and fascia system, it's a good time to install the gutters you've always needed. It's often easier to replace all materials at once rather than doing it piecemeal.

In some cases, you may not need to replace your roofing or siding to achieve your goals. Adding shutters or painting your trim a vibrant color can brighten up your exterior. Some basic maintenance can increase the life span of your roofing and siding. If you notice leaks on your ceilings or walls, don't automatically assume the roofing or siding needs replacing. Sometimes, flashing or caulking is all that's needed.

The following pages show common exterior problems. If some of these look familiar, evaluate your house to determine what's needed to fix the problem.

Tips for Identifying Problems

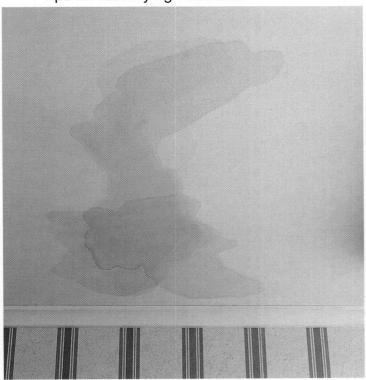

Ceiling stains show up on interior surfaces, but they're usually caused by leaks in the roof.

When shingles start to cup, or show signs of widespread damage, they need to be replaced.

Loose flashing can be caused by external forces, such as high winds, or by the failure of the sealant or fasteners. The flashing can usually be repaired or replaced without replacing the shingles.

Damaged and deteriorated flashing can cause roof leaks. The damaged piece or pieces need to be removed and replaced.

(continued next page)

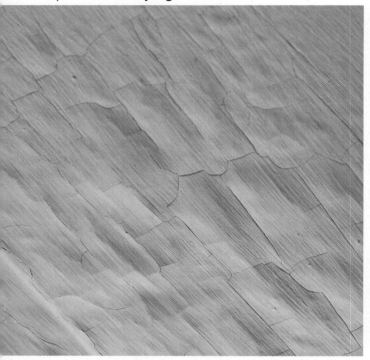

Blistering or peeling paint can be scraped off, then the wood can be painted.

Damaged panels of siding can be removed individually, rather than replacing the entire siding. The new panels are then painted to match surrounding areas.

Buckled siding happens to manufactured siding that's nailed incorrectly or when the expansion gaps are too small to allow for adequate movement. The siding needs to be removed and either renailed or trimmed to the proper size, then reinstalled.

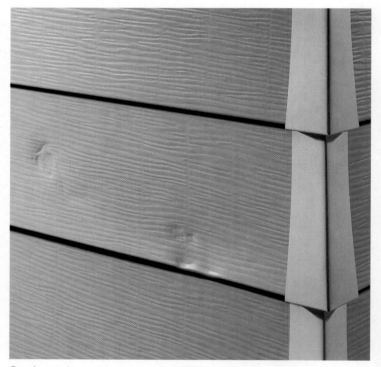

Surface damage to metal siding is difficult to repair, and cosmetic repairs often look worse than the damage. If the damage is widespread, the siding will need to be replaced.

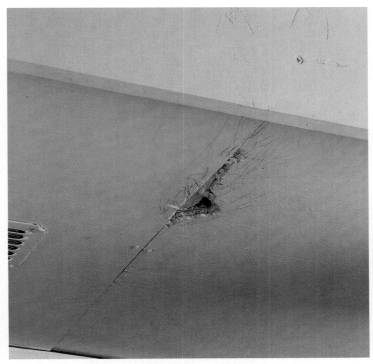

Rot and pest damage are the primary enemies of soffits. Small spots of damage can be repaired by replacing the damaged area. Widespread damage will require a new soffit system.

Rotten fascia is easy to spot from the ground on homes without a gutter system. If your house has gutters, check behind them for rot, especially if the gutters are sagging.

Leaking gutters usually result from holes or separated joints. Leaky joints can be caulked and reassembled, and holes can be patched.

Damaged gutter sections should be patched or replaced. If the damage is widespread, replace the entire gutter system.

Choosing Roofing & Siding

With so many options, choosing a roofing or siding material for your home can seem like a daunting task. Appearance, cost, ease of installation, life span, value, and maintenance all play a role. Prioritize what factors are important to you, and make your decisions accordingly. Are you willing to pay more for a cedar shake roof, or will you be content with a less-expensive asphalt shingle that imitates shakes? Are you willing to paint your wood siding every seven to ten years, or do you prefer a maintenance-free exterior?

Even after you've narrowed your decision down to a type of material, you'll still need to choose a style and color. For example, asphalt roofing is available in a seemingly endless number of colors and styles, from red scallops to green dimensional to gray three-tab shingles. Vinyl siding colors are constantly changing, and the styles range from Dutch lap to double 3" clapboard, to shakes, to board and batten.

Architectural features on the house, and even other materials already installed on the house, can help in your decision making. Stucco siding and clay roofing are a natural fit. Brick siding and metal roofing complement each other. Vinyl siding and asphalt shingles are a popular combination.

Because most roof and siding materials last for decades, you'll be living with your decision for a very long time. Take your time looking at different products, weighing their advantages and any disadvantages, before finalizing your decision.

Photo courtesy of Jame Hardie® Siding Products

Price

For most homeowners, the cost of materials is one of the deciding factors in selecting roofing or siding.

Prices are as varied as the products themselves and can differ from region to region. When adding up the costs for your project, consider everything you'll need to complete the job—not just the main roofing or siding materials. In most cases, you'll also need to purchase flashing, trim, and fasteners.

Depending on your tool arsenal, you may need to buy new tools. Some installation processes require specialty tools that you probably wouldn't otherwise have. If you're installing clay roofing,

you'll need a diamond saw blade. For brick or stucco siding, mason's tools are needed. Shipping and delivery charges, and special-order costs, can also impact your budget. Find out about these costs before settling on a product.

Slate, clay, and copper are generally the most expensive roofing products, followed by metal, cedar shakes and shingles, organic asphalt, fiberglass asphalt, and then roll roofing. Brick and stone are at the high end of the siding price scale, followed by stucco, fiber cement, wood shakes and shingles, wood lap, and vinyl, in that order.

If you're married to a particular look but can't afford the material, consider less expensive

substitutes. The look and features of many premium roofing and siding products are now replicated in other materials. Some metal roofs mimic the more expensive slate, and some asphalt shingles look like the higher priced wood shakes. For siding, one of the least-expensive products—vinyl—is now designed to imitate wood lap, wood shingles, or wood scallops. In some cases, just changing the species of wood can save a significant cost. For example, log cabin siding in pine is much more affordable than the same cabin siding in cedar.

It's important to shop around and compare prices. Visit distribution centers, lumberyards, and home improvement stores to find the best deals.

Price Comparison

	Roofing	Siding
Most Expensive	Slate	Brick
	Clay	Stone
	Copper	Stucco
	Metal	Fiber cement
	Cedar shakes/shingles	Wood shakes
	Asphalt	Wood shingles
	Roll roofing	Wood lap
Least Expensive		Vinyl

Vinyl siding and asphalt shingles require very little maintenance. They can be used on any type of home, including this Victorian.

Photo courtesy of Alcoa Home Exteriors, Inc.

Maintenance

The amount of maintenance each product requires is another important factor when choosing roofing and siding materials. Some products are virtually maintenance free, while others require regular upkeep. Decide how much time and effort you're willing to invest in maintaining your roofing and siding, and purchase materials that meet your criteria.

Maintenance tends to be more of a factor for siding than for roofing. The thought of having to paint the exterior every seven to ten years turns a lot of homeowners away from wood siding products. For others, painting is an opportunity to change the color of the house every decade or so. The amount of maintenance a siding requires is not necessarily reflected in its cost since products at both ends of the price scale, brick at the high end and vinyl at the low end, need little or no maintenance.

Older types of stucco were known to chip and crack, and needed regular maintenance. Today's stucco products use epoxy, eliminating the chipping and cracking. If the final coat of stucco is tinted to the color you want, you won't even have to paint it. Once it's installed, stucco rarely needs any maintenance. Brick and stone sidings also require little maintenance, although the mortar joints may eventually need to be filled with new mortar. Likewise, vinyl siding is maintenance free, which is part of its appeal.

Wood siding products need the most attention. A coat of paint, stain, or sealer is usually needed every seven to ten years, and that task involves a lot of preparation work, such as scraping and sanding. Fiber cement siding also needs to be repainted, but not as often. Fifteen years is the standard time frame between paint jobs.

In general, maintenance for roofing materials is fairly minimal. It's usually the result of damage to roofing components, such as torn or cracked shingles, or a break in the metal flashing. Metal, tile, and clay roofs will probably never need any maintenance. Individual asphalt shingles and wooden shakes and shingles periodically become loose, in which case they can simply be renailed. Roll roofing can develop blisters or small holes, which can be repaired with roofing cement and patches of roll roofing.

All roofing and siding products can benefit from an occasional power washing. This helps keep the exterior clean, can increase the life span of products, and enables you to identify potential trouble areas.

Siding Maintenance

Material (Siding)	Maintenance	Type of Maintenance
Vinyl	Low	Occasional cleaning
Brick	Low	Filling mortar joints
Stone	Low	Filling mortar joints
Stucco	Low	Fix cracks/chips
Fiber cement	Medium	Painting
Wood shakes	Medium	Painting/staining
Wood shingles	Medium	Painting/staining
Wood lap	High	Painting

Durability

Consider the life span of the products that you want to install on your roof or exterior walls. Some materials are extremely durable and guaranteed to last 50 years or more, while others need to be replaced in as few as 12 years.

The longevity of some products is influenced by your geographic location. Salt air along the coasts has been notoriously damaging to wood siding products, and areas subjected to high winds are prone to roofing and siding materials blowing off. The way you care for your exterior also impacts it's longevity. If you regularly paint your wood siding, immediately repair any roofing or siding damage, and follow the manufacturer's guidelines for each product, the materials will last longer.

Roofing: Slate, concrete, and clay tile are the most durable roofing products. They're heavier than other materials, and usually have a lifetime warranty. Some slate and clay roofs have been known to last hundreds of years. Metal roofs, despite their light weight, are remarkably durable. Warranties vary by product and manufacturer, but warranties of 50 years or more are becoming standard.

Since wood shakes are available in different grades, their durability also differs. Top-quality shakes carry 50-year warranties, while the lower end shakes last about 30 years. The life span of asphalt shingles also varies widely. They should last a minimum of 20 years, with the thicker, more durable architectural shingles guaranteed for up to 50 years. Roll roofing has the shortest life span, lasting between 6 and 12 years.

Siding: Brick is generally considered the most durable product, and it can carry a warranty of more than 100 years. Stone and stucco sidings are also noted for their durability, and they generally carry 50-year warranties. Fifty-year warranties are standard for fiber cement siding, too.

Although the life span of wood siding varies, depending on species of wood, climate conditions, and amount of home-owner maintenance, you should expect wood siding to last a minimum of 20 years. Some wood sidings can last well over 50 years. Vinyl siding is available in different thicknesses, from 0.035" to 0.055", with the thicker siding being the more durable and carrying lifetime warranties. The lighter weight vinyl sidings are usually guaranteed to last between 30 and 50 years.

Brick is the most durable siding, and it can last over 100 years.

Asphalt shingles and vinyl siding are a popular combination due to their low cost and good durability. Both products last 20 to 50 years.

Decorative elements give this stately home a whimsical appearance. The two-tone shingles mimic the look of old-world tile and have angled cuts at the ends to give the roof a strong visual appeal, while the trim moldings provide horizontal lines to contrast with the uniform stucco.

Roofing & Siding Styles

The type, style, and architectural features of your house all play an important role in determining which roofing and siding products will look best. Some products are natural fits for certain styles of homes, such as clay roof tiles for Mediterranean homes, and wood shingles or scallops for Victorian homes. Other products, such as asphalt shingles and lap siding, are commonplace on just about every style of home.

If you're not quite sure which roofing or siding to install, or you'd like to be reassured as to how a product will look on a finished house, drive around your neighborhood and look at homes that are similar to yours. When you find a product you like, find out what it is. If you have trouble finding homes like yours, or you want to try a newer product that hasn't been used in your area, check manufacturers' literature or websites, where you can see photos of the product on homes.

Thanks to a much broader range of roofing and siding materials now on the market, it's possible to achieve a desired look in more than one product. For example, one type of metal roof looks like slate, and some vinyl products replicate the look of wood shakes. Once you know the look you want, shop around to find the product that best suits your price range and offers an authenticity you can be happy with.

Stone and stucco siding enhance the characteristics of this elegant home. The copper roof over the bay windows easily blends with the siding, while the asphalt shingles on the main roof offer the random, rugged look of wood shakes.

The uneven edges of the siding give the appearance of wood shingles, which is the traditional siding for seaside shingle homes. However, this siding isn't really wood. It's panels of fiber cement.

Log siding transforms cabins, cottages, and ranch houses into log homes. The distinctive siding offers a rustic, frontier look.

The clay tile roof and the stucco siding complement each other on this Mediterranean-style house. The parallel lines on the roof are offset by the solid surface of the walls.

33

A combination of lap siding and scallops is common on Victorian homes, as is the decorative trim along the porch. The dimensional shingles give the roof the appearance of depth, adding to the overall persona of the home.

Brick siding is the standard for executive-style houses. The brick helps the house look solid and imposing.

Board and batten siding creates a series of vertical lines and is often used in conjunction with other types of siding, such as the shakes and scallops shown here. The different sidings break the walls into separate sections.

A touch of brick along the foundation topped by a soft vinyl siding is part of the charm of this house. The red roof adds yet another color to the vibrant facade.

With such a prominent roof, the shingles play a major role in the exterior's aesthetics. The scallop-shaped shingles provide an ornate design, and their rich color breathes life into the home's appearance.

The sleek look of this home is largely due to its metal roof. The roof looks similar to slate, but is composed of metal panels. The roof's dark color provides the perfect balance with the light-colored siding.

Vertical siding helps short structures appear taller. The vertical lines created by the vinyl siding make this entryway look taller than it really is.

Exterior trim contributes to the home's curb appeal. This wide, fluted corner trim and the wide trim around the garage contrast nicely with the Dutch lap siding.

Calculate the roof's surface by multiplying the height of the roof by the width. Do this for each section, then add the totals together. Divide that number by 100, add 10 percent for waste, and that's the number of squares of roofing materials you need.

Ordering Roofing Materials

Roofing materials are ordered in squares, with one square equaling 100 sq. ft. To determine how many squares are needed, first figure out the square footage of your roof. The easiest way to make this calculation is to multiply the length by the width of each section of roof, and add the numbers together.

For steep roofs and those with complex designs, do your measuring from the ground and multiply by a number based on the slope of your roof. Measure the length and width of your house, include the overhangs, then multiply the numbers together to determine the overall square footage. Using the chart at the right, multiply the square footage by a number based on the roof's slope (see page 56 for how to calculate the slope of your roof).

Add 10% for waste, then divide the total square footage by 100 to determine the number of squares you need. Don't spend time calculating and subtracting the areas that won't be covered, such as skylights and chimneys. They're usually small enough that they don't impact the number of squares you need. Besides, it's good to have extra materials for waste, mistakes, and later repairs.

To determine how much flashing you'll need, measure the length of the valley to figure valley flashing, the lengths of the eaves and rakes to figure drip edge, and the number and size of vent pipes to figure vent flashing.

Conversion Chart

Slope	Multiply by	Slope	Multiply by
2 in 12	1.02	8 in 12	1.20
3 in 12	1.03	9 in 12	1.25
4 in 12	1.06	10 in 12	1.30
5 in 12	1.08	11 in 12	1.36
6 in 12	1.12	12 in 12	1.41
7 in 12	1.16		

Estimate the amount of siding you'll need by calculating the square footage of each wall, then adding the numbers together. To determine the square footage of a wall, multiply the wall length by the wall height.

Ordering Siding Materials

Siding is sold by the linear foot, square foot, board foot, or square, depending on the type of material. To determine the amount of siding materials you'll need, you'll first need to calculate the square footage of each wall, then add them together to get your total surface area.

To figure the square footage for a wall, multiply the length of the wall by the height. Calculate the area on the gable end of a wall by using the formula for triangles, which is one-half the length of the base multiplied by the height of the triangle. You won't need to subtract for areas covered by windows and doors, and you won't need to add an extra 10% for waste. The window and door areas are roughly equal to the amount of waste you'll need.

Use your height and length measurements from the walls to determine how many feet of starter strip, channels, corner posts, and trim you'll

need. Keep in mind you'll probably also need to apply trim or channels around all of your doors and windows.

Depending on the siding material you're ordering, you may need extra material to allow for overlap. For example, if you want to install 10" lap siding with an 8" exposure, you'll need to account for a 2" overlap for each board. Likewise, the exposure rate for wood shakes or shingles will determine how many squares you'll need. Depending on the exposure rate, one square of shingles could cover 80 sq. ft, 100 sq. ft, or even 120 sq. ft. Most manufacturers have charts that show how much material is needed to cover a specified number of square feet at various rates of exposure. If you have trouble estimating how much material you need to purchase, ask your supplier for help.

Shingles

Roof sheathing

Ridge board

Skylight header

Rafter

Header

Jack stud

King stud

Load-bearing wall

Top plate

Header

Sole plate

Joist

Rough sill

Rim joist

Subfloor

Support beam

Studs

Joist

Foundation

Support posts

Anatomy of a House

Roofing or siding your house requires that you familiarize yourself with a few basic elements of home construction and remodeling. Take some time, before you begin, to get comfortable with the terminology of the models shown on these two pages. The understanding you will gain in this section will make it easier to plan your project, buy the right materials, and understand how roofing and siding systems work structurally.

If your project includes modifying exterior walls or the roof, you must determine if your house was built using platform- or balloon-style framing. The framing style of your home determines the location of solid framing members for nailing roofing and siding materials. If you have trouble determining what type of framing was used in your home, refer to the original blueprints, if you

Platform Framing

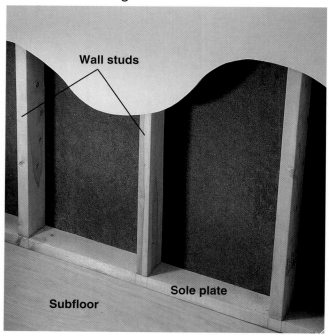

Wall studs

Sole plate

Subfloor

Platform framing (left and above) is identified by the floor-level sole plates and ceiling-level top plates to which the wall studs are attached. Most houses built after 1930 use platform framing. If you do not have access to unfinished areas, you can remove the wall surface at the bottom of a wall to determine what kind of framing was used in your home.

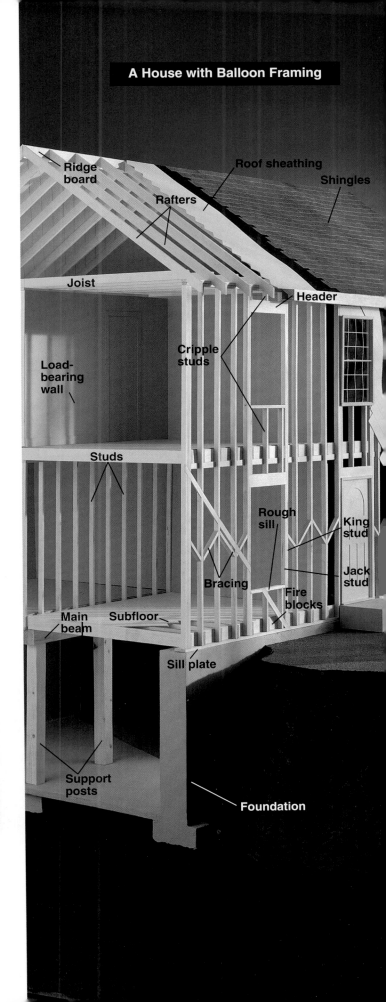

Ridge board

Rafters

Roof sheathing

Shingles

Joist

Header

Cripple studs

Load-bearing wall

Studs

Rough sill

King stud

Bracing

Jack stud

Fire blocks

Main beam

Subfloor

Sill plate

Support posts

Foundation

have them, or consult a building contractor or licensed home inspector.

Most siding products need to be nailed to wall studs. Wall sheathing typically doesn't have the strength or durability to support siding materials over an extended period of time.

Roof construction for both types of houses is pretty much the same, although balloon framed homes, because they're usually older, tend to have sheathing composed of individual boards, while platform framed homes often have sheets of sheathing. Roof sheathing must be nailed to rafters, but the roofing materials can be nailed to the sheathing. If you want to use a heavy roofing material, such as clay or concrete, you may need additional support for your roof.

Balloon Framing

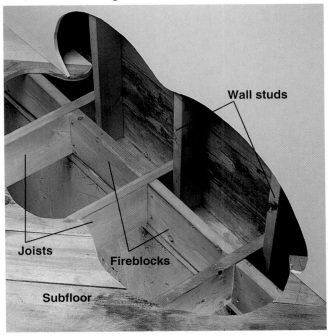

Wall studs

Joists

Fireblocks

Subfloor

Balloon framing (right and above) is identified by wall studs that run uninterrupted from the roof to a sill plate on the foundation, without the sole plates and top plates found in platform-framed walls (opposite page). Balloon framing was used in houses built before 1930.

Working Safely

Working on the exterior of the house presents challenges not faced in the interior, such as dealing with the weather, working at heights, and staying clear of power lines. By taking a few commonsense safety precautions, you can perform exterior work safely.

Dress appropriately for the job and weather. Avoid working in extreme temperatures, hot or cold, and never work outdoors during a storm or high winds.

Work with a helper whenever possible—especially when working at heights. If you must work alone, tell a family member or friend so the person can check in with you periodically. If you own a portable phone, keep it with you at all times.

Don't use tools or work at heights after consuming alcohol. If you're taking medicine, read the label and follow the recommendations regarding the use of tools and equipment.

When using ladders, extend the top of the ladder three feet above the roof edge for greater stability. Climb on and off the ladder at a point as close to the ground as possible. Use caution and keep your center of gravity low when moving from a ladder onto a roof. Keep your hips between the side rails when reaching over the side of a ladder, and be careful not to extend yourself too far or it could throw off your balance. Move the ladder as often as necessary to avoid overreaching. Finally, don't exceed the work-load rating for your ladder. Read and follow the load limits and safety instructions listed on the label.

Wear protective clothing when working outdoors, including work gloves, full-length pants, and a long-sleeved shirt. Also wear a cap to protect against direct sunlight, a particle mask when sanding, and eye protection when working with tools or chemicals. A tool organizer turns a 5-gallon bucket into a safe and convenient container for transporting tools.

Use a GFCI extension chord when working outdoors. GFCIs (Ground-fault Circuit-interrupters) shut off power if a short circuit occurs.

Tips for Working Safely

Use cordless tools to eliminate the hazards of extension cords, especially when working from ladders.

Attach a fastener to the top of your ladder for tying off air hoses. Drill a hole and secure a cap bolt to the ladder with a nut and bolt. Do not tie knots in the hoses.

Tips for Using Scaffolds

Use scaffolding for projects that require you to work at heights for long periods of time. If you rent scaffolding, be sure to get assembly instructions from the rental center.

Use plywood blocking to level and stabilize the legs of the scaffolding. If the scaffolding has wheels, lock them securely with the hand brakes.

Tips for Using Ladders

Exercise extreme caution when working near power cables. Use fiberglass or wood ladders and only work near them when absolutely necessary.

Use an extension ladder when making quick repairs to gutters, fascia, and soffits, and for gaining access to roofs.

Stabilize your ladder with stakes driven into the ground, behind each ladder foot. Install sturdy blocking under the legs of the ladder if the ground is uneven.

Fly hooks

CAUTION: Use care when approaching transition steps between flies

Make sure both fly hooks are secure before climbing an extension ladder. The open ends of the hooks should grip a rung on the lower fly extension.

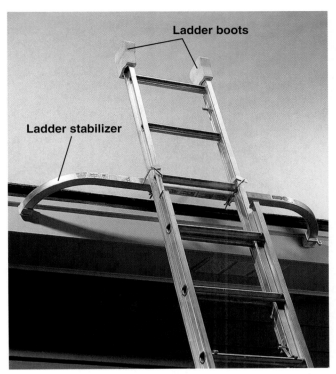

Attach an adjustable ladder stabilizer to your ladder to minimize the chance of slipping. Rest the feet of the stabilizer against broad, flat, stable surfaces.

Anchor an extension ladder by tying the top to a secure area, such as a chimney, or a securely mounted screw eye.

Tips for Using Ladder Planks

Attach a ladder jack to your ladder by slipping the rung mounts over the ladder rungs. Level the platform body arm, and lock it into place.

Set the plank in place on the platform arm. Adjust the arm's end stop to hold the plank in place.

Preparing the Job Site

Cover external air conditioning units, appliances, and other structures near the house. Make sure the power is turned off before covering them, and don't use them while they're covered.

Before starting any work, invest some time preparing the job site. Not only will this give you more room to work, it will help protect your new siding or paint job as well as preserve your landscaping and plants around the house.

This preparation work involves covering the ground around your house with plastic, tarps, or drop cloths to catch debris, especially nails, that inevitably end up on the ground during the project. When the work is finished, the debris will be contained, making cleanup a breeze.

These coverings are especially important for painting jobs. Regardless of how careful you are, paint droplets are bound to end up on your steps, sidewalks, and landscaping ornaments, so you'll need to cover them. Placing a covering on the ground is a lot quicker and easier than scraping off paint at the end of the job.

Tying up the branches on your shrubs or covering them with tarps protects them from falling debris. Tying back the branches also gives you extra space to maneuver, and prevents the plants from rubbing against your freshly painted siding. When covering plants, use tarps or drop cloths. Plastic can create a greenhouse effect, causing the plants to overheat.

Be sure to use a protective covering that won't tear when you walk on it. Because the surfaces can become slick, it's not safe to set ladders on top of them. Instead, secure your ladder in place first, then set the protective covering around it.

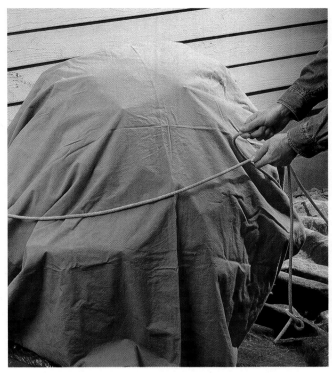

Cover plants and shrubs with tarps, rather than plastic. Tarps are less likely to tear or puncture from branches, and they won't cause the plants to overheat.

Remove exterior shutters and decorative trim to protect them from damage and make it easier to paint.

Rent a dumpster and have it on-site during the demolition phase of the project. This allows you to immediately dispose of waste, making the job site safer and cleaner.

Create a tool platform with sawhorses and a piece of plywood. Tools spread on the ground are a safety hazard and moisture can damage them. It's safer and more efficient to organize your tools so they're dry and easy to find.

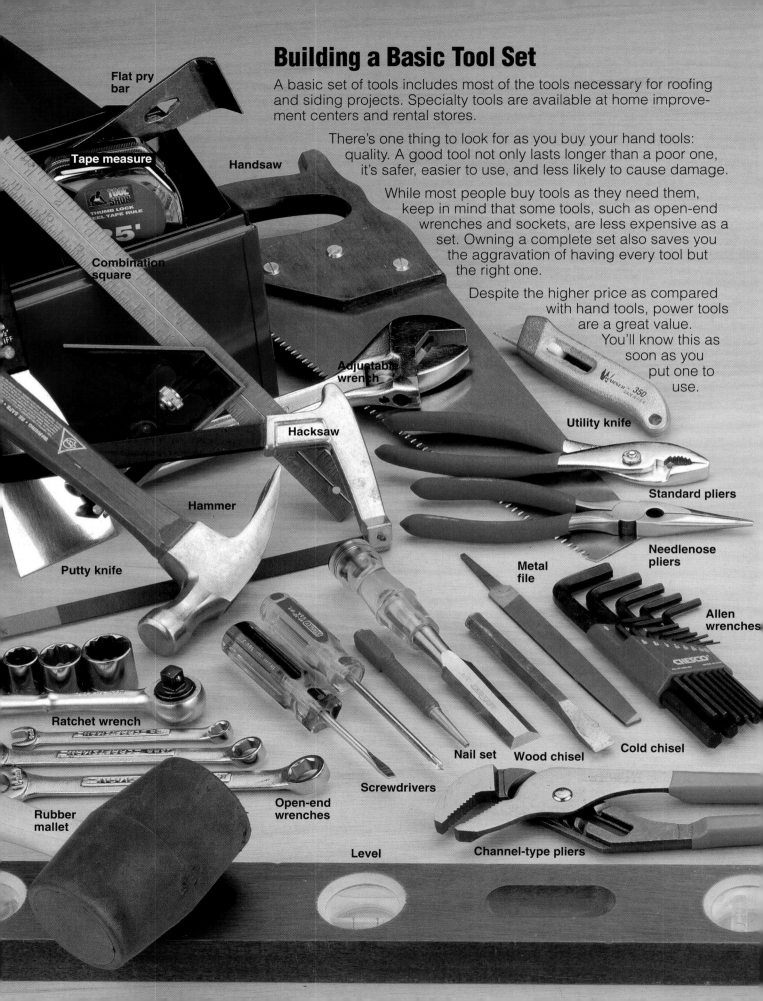

Building a Basic Tool Set

A basic set of tools includes most of the tools necessary for roofing and siding projects. Specialty tools are available at home improvement centers and rental stores.

There's one thing to look for as you buy your hand tools: quality. A good tool not only lasts longer than a poor one, it's safer, easier to use, and less likely to cause damage.

While most people buy tools as they need them, keep in mind that some tools, such as open-end wrenches and sockets, are less expensive as a set. Owning a complete set also saves you the aggravation of having every tool but the right one.

Despite the higher price as compared with hand tools, power tools are a great value. You'll know this as soon as you put one to use.

Flat pry bar

Tape measure

Handsaw

Combination square

Adjustable wrench

Utility knife

Hacksaw

Standard pliers

Hammer

Needlenose pliers

Putty knife

Metal file

Allen wrenches

Ratchet wrench

Nail set

Wood chisel

Cold chisel

Screwdrivers

Open-end wrenches

Rubber mallet

Level

Channel-type pliers

The time it takes to complete repetitive tasks, such as drilling, sawing, and sanding, is reduced dramatically by a good power tool. For many jobs, power tools are more accurate and easier to use than their manual counterparts—try using a handsaw to make a straight cut through plywood, for example.

For roofing and siding projects, you won't need a fully equipped workshop, but a few of the standard tools will come in handy. A circular saw is ideal for any straight cuts in siding and sheathing; jig saws cut curves, holes, and slots in most materials; a palm sander makes short work of laborious sanding tasks for painting; cordless screwdrivers are quick on screws and easy on your wrists when you install metal roofing; and a cordless drill, with a keyless chuck and adjustable speed, is one of the handiest power tools available.

In addition to these tools, you'll need some specialty tools for installing roofing and siding, such as aviation snips, roofer's hatchet, hammer stapler, T-bevel, miter saw, special saw blades, and, to make the job go much faster, a pneumatic nailer and air compressor.

Circular saw

Palm sander

Jig saw

Cordless screwdriver

Cordless drill

Roofing Installation

The roof structure is overlaid with lapped courses of material that serve the same function as scales on a fish or feathers on a bird, although the installation techniques are as varied as the roofs themselves. For example, clay tiles have a unique overlapping pattern to dispel water, metal roofing has locking channels and is installed similar to vinyl siding, and asphalt shingles are aligned according to tab slots and nailed in place. Every technique does share a common goal—to make the roof watertight.

Every roof also needs to be installed on a flat, solid surface. If your roof decking is damaged, you'll need to replace the sheathing before applying any new roofing materials.

This section discusses removing your old roof covering, installing underlayment and flashing, and installing the new roof. Before starting the job, read through the sections that apply to your project and familiarize yourself with all of the processes.

Work in small sections of the roof at a time, unless you can tear off the old covering and install the new roof within a day or two. You'll want to keep your roof covered as much as possible because it is quite vulnerable between the time the old covering is removed and the new one is installed.

49

Roofing Basics

The elements of a roof system work together to provide shelter, drainage, and ventilation. The roof covering is composed of sheathing, felt paper, and shingles. Metal flashing is attached in valleys and around chimneys, vent pipes, and other roof elements to seal out water. Soffits cover and protect the eaves area below the roof overhang. Fascia, usually attached at the ends of the rafters, supports soffit panels as well as a gutter and downspout system. Soffit vents and roof vents keep fresh air circulating throughout the roof system.

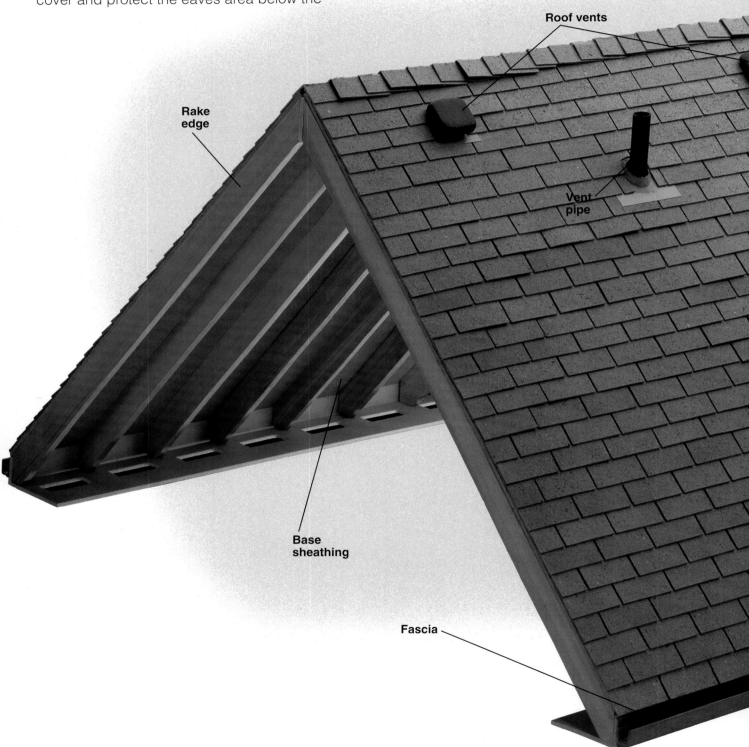

Roof vents

Rake edge

Vent pipe

Base sheathing

Fascia

Valley flashing

Counter-flashing

Ridge

Shingles

Base flashing

Soffit vents

Soffit panel

Valley

Eave

Gutters

Types of Roofing

Asphalt shingles are comprised of roofing felt saturated with asphalt and imbedded with a layer of mineral granules. Asphalt shingles are the most common roofing material, and they can be easily installed and repaired by homeowners.

Wood shingles are usually made of western red cedar. They're thinner, smaller, and less expensive than wood shakes. Many people admire the beauty of wood shingles. In addition to their beauty, they're durable (especially when treated with a preservative every 3 to 5 years) and easy to install.

Vertical metal roofing has evolved from the terne and copper of days gone by to the corrugated aluminum or galvanized steel panels most frequently used today. Usually painted, it's attractive, durable, and moderately priced.

Horizontal metal roofs have been associated in the past with tin-covered storage sheds or copper-domed cathedrals, but today's panels of corrugated aluminum or galvanized steel are practical and attractive options.

Photo courtesy of Vande Hey Raleigh

Slate is a natural stone. The shingles are made from blocks of slate that are split into shingles. Beautiful, durable, and fireproof, slate's primary drawbacks are its cost and weight.

Clay tiles are fireproof and provide a distinctive appearance. They offer virtually the same benefits and drawbacks as slate, but create a very different look. Heavy and relatively expensive, they're also weather-resistant and insect-proof. Clay tiles are available in several different patterns.

Built-up roofs are made from alternating layers of roofing felt and hot tar, covered with a protective layer of gravel. Built-up roofs are more commonly found on commercial buildings than homes, but they're well suited for houses with flat roofs or roofs with a slope of less than 3-in-12.

Photo courtesy of GAF Materials Corporation

Roll roofing is an asphalt roofing material that's rolled onto the roof. Like built-up roofs, roll roofing is primarily used on flat roofs or roofs with a slight slope. It's quick and easy to install, but has a short life span.

Tools & Materials

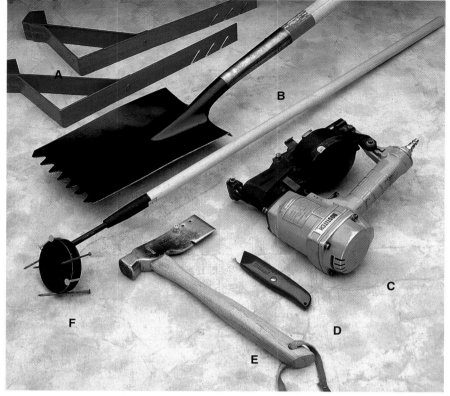

Specialty roofing tools include: roof jacks (A), roofing shovel (B), pneumatic nailer (C), utility knife with hooked blade (D), roofing hammer with alignment guides and hatchet blade (E), and a release magnet for site cleanup (F).

Working conditions on a roof can be arduous, so make the job as easy as possible by gathering the right tools and equipment before you begin.

Some of these tools, such as a pneumatic nailer and roofer's hatchet, are specific to roofing projects. If you don't have them and don't want to buy them, you can rent them from a rental center.

Use roof jacks on steep roofs. Nail the supports at the fourth or fifth course of shingles, and add the widest board the supports will hold.

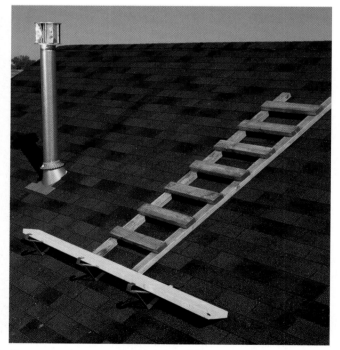

For more secure footing, fashion a roofing ladder by nailing wood strips across a pair of 2 × 4s. Secure the ladder to the roof jacks, and use it to maintain your footing.

Rolled flashing material

Drip edge

Preformed valley flashing

Aviation snips

Vent pipe flashing

Step flashing blanks

Skylight flashing kit (partial)

Roof flashing can be hand-cut or purchased in pre-formed shapes and sizes. Long pieces of valley flashing, base flashing, top saddles, and other non-standard pieces can be cut from rolled flashing material, using aviation snips. Step flashing blanks can be bought in standard sizes and bent to fit. Drip edge and vent pipe flashing are available preformed. Sky-light flashing usually comes as a kit with the window. Complicated flashings, such as chimney crickets, can be custom fabricated by a metalworker.

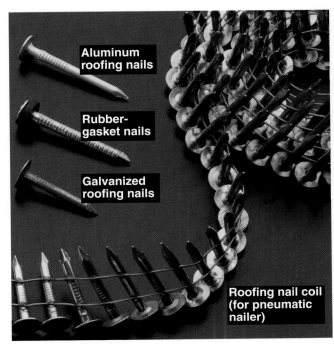

Aluminum roofing nails

Rubber-gasket nails

Galvanized roofing nails

Roofing nail coil (for pneumatic nailer)

Different fasteners are specially developed for dif-ferent jobs. Use galvanized roofing nails to hand-nail shingles; use aluminum nails for aluminum flashing; use rubber-gasket nails for galvanized metal flash-ing; and use nail coils for pneumatic nailers.

Felt paper (30#)

Roofing cement

Ice-guard membrane

Common roofing materials include 30# felt paper for use as underlayment; ice-guard membrane for use as underlayment in cold climates; and tubes of roofing cement for sealing small holes, cracks, and joints.

Dress for protection and safety when working on a roof. Wear rubber-soled shoes, knee pads, nail apron, tool belt, long-sleeved shirt, full-length pants, and work gloves. Wear protective eyewear when working with power tools.

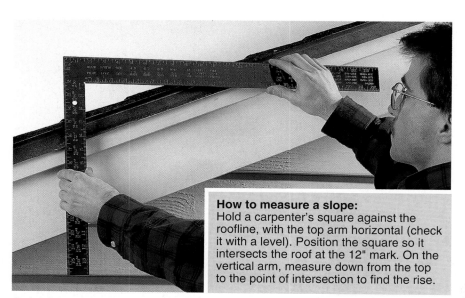

How to measure a slope:
Hold a carpenter's square against the roofline, with the top arm horizontal (check it with a level). Position the square so it intersects the roof at the 12" mark. On the vertical arm, measure down from the top to the point of intersection to find the rise.

Calculate the slope of your roof before beginning any roofing project. Roof slope is defined as the number of inches the roof rises for each 12" of horizontal extension (called the "run"). For example, the roof shown above has a 5-in-12 slope: it rises 5" in 12" of run. Knowing the slope is important when selecting materials and gauging the difficulty of working on the roof. To ensure safe footing, install temporary roof jacks if the slope is 7-in-12 or steeper. Roofs with a slope of 3-in-12 or less require a fully bonded covering to protect against the effects of pooling water.

Planning a Roofing Project

If your roof has more than one or two layers of shingles, if the shingles are buckled or cupped, or if the sheathing is buckled, you'll need to remove the old roofing completely. Wait to start the project until you've drafted a detailed plan.

Estimate the time your project will require (see chart, opposite page). Consider the slope of the roof and whether you'll need to install roof jacks. Organizing tasks in a logical sequence and dividing the project into manageable portions that can be completed in a single day saves time and inconvenience.

Measure the square footage of your roof. Shop and compare prices, then make a rough cost estimate for the shingles you select.

Count the number of roof elements, such as vent pipes, vent fans, skylights, dormers, and chimneys, and estimate the amount of flashing needed. Also include felt paper, roofing cement, and nails. Add 15 percent to your estimate to allow for waste.

Everything You Need

Tools: carpenter's square, hammer, tape measure, flat pry bar.

Materials: 16d nails, roof jacks, 2 × 8 or 2 × 10 boards.

Tips for Planning a Roofing Project

Note: All time estimates are based on one worker. Reduce time by 40% if there is a helper.

*One square =100 sq. ft.

**Include area of dormer surface in "flat run" estimate

Protect against damage from falling materials when working on the roof. Hang tarps over the sides of the house, and lean plywood against the house to protect the vegetation and siding.

How to Install Roof Jacks

1 Nail roof jacks to the roof at the fourth or fifth course. Drive 16d nails into the overlap, or dead area, where they won't be exposed. Install one jack every 4 ft., with a 6" to 12" overhang at the ends of the boards.

2 Shingle over the tops of the roof jacks. Rest a 2 × 8 or 2 × 10 board on the jacks. Fasten the board with a nail driven through the hole in the lip of each roof jack.

3 When the project is complete, remove the boards and jacks. Position the end of a flat pry bar over each nail and drive in the nail by rapping the shank with a hammer.

Rent a dumpster from a waste disposal company or your local waste management department. Position the dumpster directly below the roof edge, so when you're tearing off the old roofing materials, the debris can be dumped from the roof directly into the dumpster.

Completing the Tear-off

Removing shingles, commonly referred to in the roofing trade as the *tear-off*, can be done rather quickly. This makes it one of the more satisfying parts of a reshingling project. If you can't reshingle your entire roof in one day, tear off one section of roofing at a time, roof that section, then move on to the next part of the roof.

The tear-off produces a lot of debris and waste. A few preparatory steps make cleanup much easier. Lay tarps on the ground and lean sheets of plywood against the house to protect shrubbery and the siding.

If renting a dumpster isn't practical, set wheelbarrows on tarps as an alternative for catching debris. However, you'll still be responsible for disposing of the old roof, which will probably require several trips to the landfill. To work efficiently, have another person deal with the debris on the ground as you work on the roof.

Everything You Need

Tools: hammer, chisel, pry bar, utility knife, roofing shovel, broom, release magnet, rake, tin snips, reciprocating saw, drill.

Materials: protective gear, tarps.

How to Tear Off Old Roof Coverings

1 Remove the ridge cap, using a flat pry bar. Pry up the cap shingles at the nail locations.

TIP: *Drive staples every 6" to 12" along the edges of felt paper, and one staple per square foot in the field area.*

2 Measuring up from the eaves, make a mark 32" above the top of the last row of underlayment, and snap another chalk line. Roll out the next course of felt paper (or ice guard, if required) along the chalk line, overlapping the first course by 4".

3 At valleys, roll felt paper across from both sides, overlapping the ends by 36". Install felt paper up to the ridge—ruled side up—snapping horizontal lines every two or three rows to check alignment. Overlap horizontal seams by 4", vertical seams by 12", and hips and ridges by 6". Trim the courses flush with the rake edges.

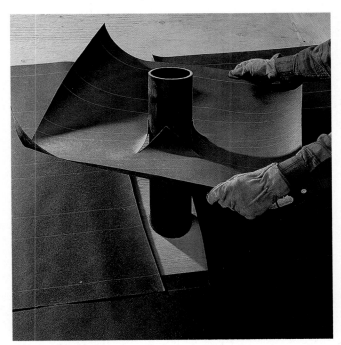

4 Apply felt paper up to an obstruction, then resume laying the course on the opposite side (making sure to maintain the line). Cut a patch that overlaps the felt paper by 12" on all sides. Make a crosshatch cutout for the obstruction. Position the patch over the obstruction, staple it in place, then caulk the seams with roofing cement.

5 At the bottom of dormers and sidewalls, tuck the felt paper under the siding where it intersects with the roof. Carefully pry up the siding and tuck at least 2" of paper under it. Also tuck the paper under counterflashing on chimneys and skylights. Leave the siding or counterflashing unfastened until after you install the step flashing.

Drip edge

Drip edge flashing protects against water working its way under the roofing materials along the eaves and rake edges of the roof.

Installing Drip Edge

Drip edge is a flashing that's installed along the eaves and rake edges of the roof to direct water away from the roof decking. Although its job is to deflect water, it also gives the edges of the roof an attractive finish. A corrosion-resistant material, drip edge won't stain your roofing materials or fascia.

The flashing is installed along the eaves before the felt paper is attached to allow water to run off the roof in the event it gets under the shingles. Drip edge is installed at the rake edges after the felt paper has been attached to keep wind-driven rain from getting under the paper.

Drip edge is always nailed directly to the roof

decking, rather than to the fascia or rake boards. The nail heads are later covered by roofing materials.

There are two basic styles of drip edge. One is the C-style drip edge that doesn't have an overhang, and the other is the extended-profile drip edge that has a hemmed overhang along the edges.

Everything You Need

Tools: hammer, tape measure, aviation snips.

Materials: drip edge, roofing nails.

64

How to Install Drip Edge

1 Cut a 45° miter at one end of the drip edge, using aviation snips. Place the drip edge along the eaves end of the roof, aligning the mitered end with the rake edge. Nail the drip edge in place every 12".

2 Overlap pieces of drip edge by 2". Install drip edge across the entire eaves, ending with a mitered cut on the opposite corner.

3 Apply felt paper, and ice guard if needed, to the roof, overhanging the eaves by ⅜" (see pages 62 to 63).

4 Cut a 45° miter in a piece of drip edge, and install it along the rake edge, forming a miter joint with the drip edge along the eaves. Overlap pieces by 2", making sure the higher piece is on top at the overlap. Apply drip edge all the way to the peak. Install drip edge along the other rake edges the same way.

Flashing is a critical component of roofs that helps keep the structure watertight. Most roofs have flashing in the valleys and around dormers. This roof uses several valley flashings as well as flashing around the window and around the bump-out in the roof.

Installing Flashing

Flashing is a metal or rubber barrier used to protect the seams around roof elements or between adjoining roof surfaces. Metal flashings are made of either galvanized steel, copper, or aluminum. Whatever metal you choose, use nails made of the same material. Mixing metals can cause corrosion and discoloration.

Flashing's primary job is to channel water off the roof and away from seams. It's installed in areas where shingles can't be applied and would otherwise be prone to leaks. Some flashing, such as the valley flashing shown on the opposite page, is installed over the underlayment, prior to the installation of the shingles. Other flashing, such as flashing for vent pipes, is installed in conjunction with the shingles, and is shown as part of the roofing sequences throughout this chapter.

While most flashing is pre-formed, you'll sometimes need to bend your own. This is especially true for flashing around roof elements, such as

chimneys and dormers, that often need to be custom fit. Building a bending jig, as shown on the opposite page, allows you to easily bend flashing to fit your needs.

When installing flashing around roof elements, the flashing should be secured to one surface only—usually the roof deck. Use only roofing cement to bond the flashing to the roof elements. Flashing must be able to flex as the roof element and the roof deck expand and contract. If the flashing is fastened to both the roof deck and roof element, it will tear or loosen.

Everything You Need

Tools: aviation snips, caulk gun, flat pry bar, roofing hammer, tape measure, trowel, clamp.

Materials: galvanized metal valley flashing, roofing cement, roofing nails or rubber-gasket nails, scrap wood, screws.

How to Bend Flashing

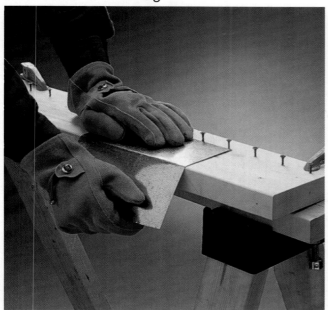

1 To bend flashing, make a bending jig by driving screws into a piece of wood, creating a space one-half the width of the flashing when measured from the edge of the board. Clamp the bending jig to a worksurface. Lay a piece of flashing flat on the board, and bend it over the edge.

2 Use the old flashing as a template for making replacement pieces. This is especially useful for reproducing complicated flashing, such as saddle flashing for chimneys and dormers.

How to Install Valley Flashing

8" overlap

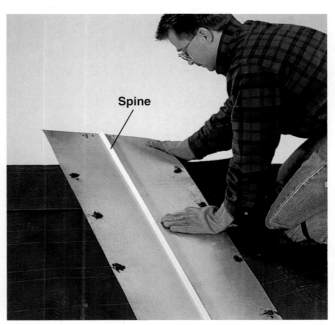

Spine

1 Starting at the eaves, set a piece of valley flashing into the valley so the bottom of the V rests in the crease of the valley. Nail the flashing at 12" intervals along each side. Trim the end of the flashing at the eaves so it's flush with the drip edge at each side. Working toward the top of the valley, add flashing pieces so they overlap by at least 8", until you reach the ridge.

2 Let the top edge of the flashing extend a few inches beyond the ridge. Bend the flashing over the ridge so it lies flat on the opposite side of the roof. If you're installing pre-formed flashing, make a small cut in the spine for easier bending. Cover nail heads with roofing cement (unless you're using rubber-gasket nails). Apply roofing cement along the side edges of the flashing.

The use of a boom truck to lift the roofing supplies onto the roof will save you the laborious task of carrying the shingles onto your roof.

Loading Your Roof

Nothing can take the enjoyment out of a roofing project faster than having to carry the roofing materials up a ladder onto the roof. Typical bundles of asphalt shingles weigh between 65 and 75 pounds, and you could need as many as 50 bundles. That's a lot of work, and then you'll need to find the energy to shingle the roof!

Fortunately, you can eliminate this backbreaking chore. For a minimal fee, most roofing suppliers will deliver the shingles directly onto the roof using a boom truck. If the supplier doesn't provide this service, you can rent a mechanical hoist from a rental supply store and transport the shingles yourself without carrying them.

Even when shingles are delivered to the roof, you'll still need to unload and stack them. To keep the materials from getting in your way as you work, stack the bundles near the peak. Make several stacks along the ridge to distribute the weight and make them easier to access when working.

Have the shingles delivered when you're ready to start the installation. You don't want the shingles sitting on top of your roof for weeks before the installation begins.

Tips for Loading a Roof

Unload the roofing materials from the hoist. Place the first bundle flat on the roof, then set the next bundles partially on the underlying bundle, and partially on the roof.

Stack bundles of shingles on various locations across the roof so they can be easily accessed during installation.

Place roofing materials at a point where two roofs intersect. This helps support the shingles and keeps them from falling off the roof.

Make several stacks of shingles near the peak to disperse the weight.

Stagger shingles for effective protection against leaks. If the tab slots are aligned in successive rows, water forms channels, increasing erosion of the mineral surface of the shingles. Creating a 6" offset between rows of shingles—with the 3-tab shingles shown above—ensures that the tab slots do not align.

Installing 3-tab Shingles

If you want to install asphalt shingles on your roof, then you're in good company. Asphalt shingles, also known as composition shingles, are the roofing of choice for nearly four out of five homeowners in America. They perform well in all types of climate, are available in a multitude of colors, shapes, and textures to complement every housing design, and are less expensive than most other roofing products.

Asphalt shingles are available as either fiberglass shingles or organic shingles. Both types are made with asphalt, the difference being that one uses a fiberglass reinforcing mat, while the other uses a cellulose-fiber mat. Fiberglass shingles are lighter, thinner, and have a better fire rating. Organic shingles have a higher tear strength, are more flexible in cold climates, and are used more often in northern regions.

Although the roofing market has exploded with innovative new asphalt shingle designs, such as

the architectural or laminated shingle that offers a three-dimensional look, the standard 3-tab asphalt shingle is still the most common, which is the project we're featuring here. The tabs provide an easy reference for aligning shingles for installation.

To help the job get done faster, rent an air compressor and pneumatic roofing gun. This will greatly reduce the time you spend nailing.

Everything You Need

Tools: aviation snips, carpenter's square, chalk line, flat bar, roofing hatchet or pneumatic nailer, utility knife, straightedge, tape measure, chalk gun.

Materials: flashing, shingles, nailing cartridges, roofing cement, ⅞" and 1¼" roofing nails, rubber-gasket nails.

How to Install 3-tab Shingles

TIP: *Use blue chalk rather than red. Red chalk will stain roofing materials.*

Full tab

Half-tab

1 Cover the roof with felt paper (pages 62 to 63) and install drip edge (pages 64 to 65). Snap a chalk line onto the felt paper or ice guard, 11½" up from the eaves edge, to mark the alignment of the starter course. This will result in a ½" shingle overhang for standard 12" shingles.

2 Trim off one-half (6") of an end tab on a shingle. Position the shingle upside down, so the tabs are aligned with the chalk line and the half-tab is flush against the rake edge. Drive ⅞" roofing nails near each end, 1" down from each slot, between tabs. Butt a full, upside-down shingle next to the trimmed shingle, and nail it. Fill out the row, trimming the last shingle flush with the opposite rake edge.

3 Apply the first full course of shingles over the starter course, with the tabs pointing down. Begin at the rake edge where you began the starter row. Place the first shingle so it overhangs the rake edge by ⅜" and the eaves edge by ½". Make sure the top of each shingle is flush with the top of the starter course, following the chalk line.

4 Snap a chalk line from the eaves edge to the ridge to create a vertical line to align the shingles. Choose an area with no obstructions, as close as possible to the center of the roof. The chalk line should pass through a slot or a shingle edge on the first full shingle course. Use a carpenter's square to establish a line perpendicular to the eaves edge.

(continued next page)

How to Install 3-tab Shingles (continued)

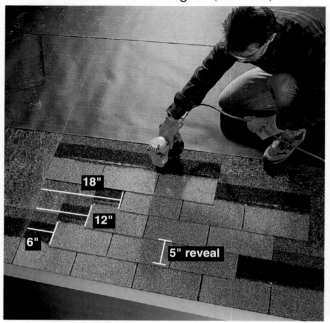

TIP: *Install roof jacks, if needed, after filling out the fifth course.*

5 Use the vertical reference line to establish a shingle pattern with slots that are offset by 6" in succeeding courses. Tack down a shingle 6" to one side of the vertical line, 5" above the bottom edge of the first-course shingles, to start the second row. Tack down shingles for the third and fourth courses, 12" and 18" from the vertical line. Butt the fifth course against the line.

6 Fill in shingles in the second through fifth courses, working upward from the second course and maintaining a consistent 5" reveal. Slide lower-course shingles under any upper-course shingles left partially nailed, and then nail them down.

7 Check the alignment of the shingles after each 4-course cycle. In several spots on the last installed course, measure from the bottom edge of a shingle to the nearest felt paper line. If you discover any misalignment, make minor adjustments over the next few rows until it's corrected.

8 When you reach obstructions, such as dormers, install a full course of shingles above them so you can retain your shingle offset pattern. On the unshingled side of the obstruction, snap another vertical reference line, using the shingles above the obstruction as a guide.

9 Shingle upward from the eaves on the unshingled side of the obstruction, using the vertical line as a reference for re-establishing your shingle slot offset pattern. Fill out the shingle courses past the rake edges of the roof, then trim off the excess.

10 Trim off excess shingle material at the V in the valley flashing, using a utility knife and straight-edge. Do not cut into the flashing. The edges will be trimmed back farther at a slight taper after both roof decks are completely shingled.

11 Install shingles on adjoining roof decks, start-ing at the bottom edge, using the same offset alignment pattern shown in steps 1 to 6. Install shin-gles until courses overlap the center of the valley flashing. Trim shingles at both sides of the valley when finished.

12 Install shingles up to the vent pipe so the flash-ing rests on at least one row of shingles. Apply a heavy, double bead of roofing cement along the bottom edge of the flange.

(continued next page)

13 Place the flashing over the vent pipe. Position the flashing collar so the longer portion of the tapered neck slopes down the roof and the flange lies over the shingles. Nail the perimeter of the flange, using rubber-gasket nails.

14 Cut shingles to fit around the neck of the flashing so they lie flat against the flange. Do not drive roofing nails through the flashing. Instead, apply roofing cement to the back of shingles where they lie over the flashing.

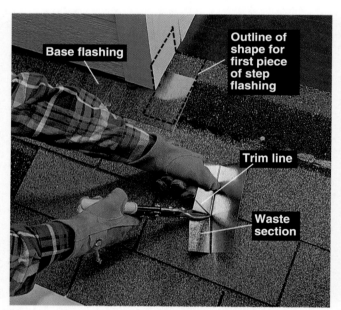

15 Shingle up to an element that requires flashing, so the top of the reveal areas are within 5" of the element. Install base flashing, using the old base flashing as a template. Bend a piece of step flashing in half and set it next to the lowest corner of the element. Mark a trim line on the flashing, following the vertical edge of the element. Cut the flashing to fit.

16 Pry out the lowest courses of siding and any trim at the base of the element. Insert spacers to prop the trim or siding away from the work area. Apply roofing cement to the base flashing in the area where the overlap with the step flashing will be formed. Tuck the trimmed piece of step flashing under the propped area, and secure the flashing. Fasten the flashing with one rubber-gasket nail driven near the top, and into the roof deck.

17 Apply roofing cement to the top side of the first piece of step flashing, where it will be covered by the next shingle course. Install the shingle by pressing it firmly into the roofing cement. Do not nail through the flashing underneath.

18 Tuck another piece of flashing under the trim or siding, overlapping the first piece of flashing at least 2". Set the flashing into roofing cement applied on the top of the shingle. Nail the shingle in place without driving nails through the flashing. Install flashing up to the top of the element the same way. Trim the last piece of flashing to fit the top corner of the element. Reattach the siding and trim.

19 Shingle up to the chimney base. Use the old base flashing as a template to cut new flashing. Bend up the counterflashing. Apply roofing cement to the base of the chimney and the shingles just below the base. Press the base flashing into the roofing cement and bend the flashing around the edges of the chimney. Drive rubber-gasket nails through the flashing flange into the roof deck.

20 Install step flashing and shingles, working up to the high side of the chimney. Fasten flashing to the chimney with roofing cement. Fold down the counterflashing as you go.

(continued next page)

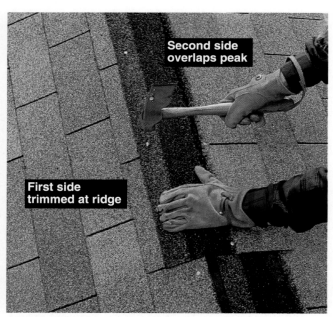

Second side overlaps peak

First side trimmed at ridge

Top flashing

21 Cut and install top flashing (also called a saddle) around the high side of the chimney. Overlap the final piece of flashing along each side. Attach the flashing with roofing cement applied to the deck and chimney, and with rubber-gasket nails driven through the flashing base into the roof deck. Shingle past the chimney, using roofing cement (not nails) to attach shingles over the flashing.

22 When you reach a hip or ridge, shingle up the first side until the top of the uppermost reveal area is within 5" of the hip or ridge. Trim the shingles along the peak. Install shingles on the opposite side of the hip or ridge. Overlap the peak no more than 5".

23 Cut three 12"-square cap shingles from each 3-tab shingle. With the back surface facing up, cut the shingles at the tab lines. Trim the top corners of each square with an angled cut, starting just below the seal strip to avoid overlaps in the reveal area.

24 Snap a chalk line 6" down from the ridge, parallel to the peak. Attach cap shingles, starting at one end of the ridge, aligned with the chalk line. Drive two 1¼" roofing nails per cap, about 1" from each edge, just below the seal strip.

25 Following the chalk line, install cap shingles halfway along the ridge, creating a 5" reveal for each cap. Then, starting at the opposite end, install caps over the other half of the ridge to meet the first run in the center. Cut a 5"-wide section from the reveal area of a shingle tab, and use it as a "closure cap" to cover the joint where the caps meet.

26 Shingle the hips in the same manner, using a chalk reference line and cap shingles. Start at the bottom of each hip and work to the peak. Where hips join with roof ridges, install a custom shingle cut from the center of a cap shingle. Set the cap at the end of the ridge, and bend the corners so they fit over the hips. Secure each corner with a roofing nail, and cover the nail heads with roofing cement.

27 After all shingles are installed, trim them at the valleys to create a gap that's 3" wide at the top and widens at a rate of ⅛" per foot as it moves downward. Use a utility knife and straightedge to cut the shingles, making sure not to cut through the valley flashing. At the valleys, seal the undersides and edges of shingles with roofing cement. Also cover exposed nail heads with roofing cement.

28 Mark and trim the shingles at the rake edges of the roof. Snap a chalk line ⅜" from the edge to make an overhang, then trim the shingles.

Shingling over existing shingles saves time, and it doesn't diminish the final appearance. Properly installed roofs look just as good over old shingles as they do when installed directly on the roof decking.

Shingling Over an Old Roof

Installing shingles over your current shingles saves you the time, labor, and expense of tearing off the old roof covering. This method certainly has its appeal, but there's still some preparation work involved. Make any necessary repairs to the roof decking before applying new shingles. Replace any missing shingles, and renail any loose ones. Drive down protruding nails so the heads won't pierce the new roofing materials.

In order to shingle over old roofing, you cannot have more than one or two layers of shingles already on the roof, depending on your building codes. If you already have the maximum number of layers, the old shingles will need to be com-

pletely removed. To check for underlying shingles, lift up the shingles along the rake or eaves end of the roof and count the number of layers.

Before starting the project, read the section on shingling a roof, pages 70 to 77.

Everything You Need

Tools: aviation snips, carpenter's square, chalk line, flat pry bar, roofing hatchet or pneumatic nailer, utility knife, straightedge, tape measure.

Materials: flashing, shingles, nailing cartridges, roofing cement, roofing nails.

How to Shingle Over an Old Roof

1 Cut tabs off shingles and install the remaining strips over the reveal area of the old first course, creating a flat surface for the starter row of new shingles. Use roofing nails that are long enough to penetrate the roof decking by at least ¾".

2 Trim the top of shingles for the first course. The shingles should be sized to butt against the bottom edge of the old third course, overhanging the roof edge by ½". Install shingles so the tab slots don't align with the slots in the old shingles.

TIP: Valley flashing in good condition does not have to be replaced. Replace any other old flashing as you go.

3 Using the old shingles to direct your layout, begin installing the new shingles. Maintain a consistent tab/slot offset. Shingle up toward the roof ridge, stopping before the final course. Install flashing as you proceed.

4 Flashing is installed using the same techniques and materials as shingling over felt paper, except that you need to trim or fill in shingles around vent pipes and roof vents to create a flat surface for the base flange of the flashing pieces.

5 Tear off old hip and ridge caps before shingling these areas. Replace with new ridge caps after all other shingling has been completed.

79

Installing Cedar Shakes

Cedar shakes—which are thick and rough—and shingles—which are tapered and smooth—are installed in much the same way, with one major difference. Shakes have felt paper installed between each course, while shingles do not. Shingles are often applied over open sheathing, while shakes are installed over open or solid sheathing. Air circulation under shakes and shingles can increase their life span. Check your local building codes to see what type of sheathing is recommended for your area.

The gaps between shakes and shingles, called

joints, are specified by the manufacturer. You can determine how much of the material to leave exposed below the overlap, as long as it falls within the manufacturer's guidelines.

Everything You Need

Tools: roofer's hatchet, tape measure, utility knife, stapler, chalk line, circular saw, jig saw, caulk gun.

Materials: shakes, flashing, nails, 30# felt paper, stapler, mason's string, roofing cement.

Cedar Shakes & Shingles

Wood shakes and shingles are available in different grades. Some of the more popular include: resawn shake (A), No. 1 hand-split medium shake (B), standard-grade shake (C), taper-sawn shake (D), No. 1 heavy shake (E), CCA treated medium shake (F), No. 2 shingle (G), undercoursing shingle (H), No. 1 shingle (I).

Roof Decking for Cedar Shakes & Shingles

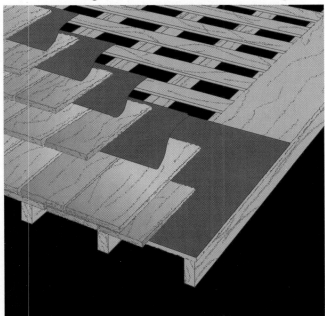

Spaced sheathing is common, and sometimes required, for cedar shakes and shingles. The sheathing is solid along the eaves and rake ends, and spaced in the field to allow for air circulation.

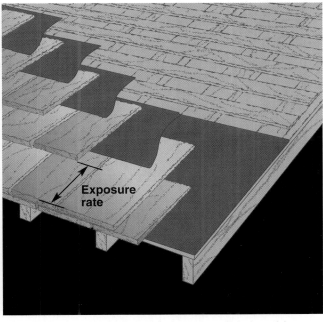

To install spaced sheathing over solid sheathing, place 2 × 4s flat over each rafter and nail them to the roof. Nail 1 × 4 or 1 × 6 nailing strips across the 2 × 4s. Keep the strips together along the eaves, then space them at a distance equal to the exposure rate in the field.

How to Install Cedar Shakes

1 Prepare the roof decking by installing valley flashing at all valleys (pages 66 to 67). Apply felt paper underlayment to the first 36" of the roof deck. Note: Depending on your climate and building codes, you may want to install ice and water shield for this step rather than felt paper.

2 Install a starter shake so it overhangs the eaves and rake edge by 1½". Do the same on the opposite side of the roof. Run a taut string between the bottom edges of the two shakes. Install the remaining shakes in the starter row, aligning the bottoms with the string. Keep the manufacturer's recommended distance between shakes, usually ⅜" to ⅝".

TIP: *Set the gauge on your roofer's hatchet to the exposure rate. You can then use the hatchet as a quick reference for checking the exposure.*

3 Set the first course of shakes over the starter row, aligning the shakes along the rake ends and bottoms. Joints between shakes must overlap by at least 1½". Drive two nails in each shake, ¾" to 1" from the edges, and 1½" to 2" above the exposure line. Use the hatchet to rip shakes to fit.

4 Snap a chalk line over the first course of shakes at the exposure line. Snap a second line at a distance that's twice the exposure rate. Staple an 18"-wide strip of felt paper at the second line. Overlap felt paper vertical seams by 4". Install the second course of shakes at the exposure line, offsetting joints by 1½" minimum. Install remaining courses the same way.

5 Set shakes in place along valleys, but don't nail them. Hold a 1 × 4 against the center of the valley flashing without nailing it. Place it over the shakes to use as a guide for marking the angle of the valley. Cut the shakes, using a circular saw, then install.

6 Use the 1 × 4 to align the edge of the shakes along the valley. Keep the 1 × 4 butted against the valley center, and place the edge of the shake along the edge of the board. Avoid nailing through the valley flashing when installing the shakes.

7 Notch shakes to fit around a plumbing stack, using a jig saw, then install a course of shakes below the stack. Apply roofing cement to the underside of the stack flashing, then place it over the stack and over the shakes. Nail the flashing along the edges.

8 Overlap the exposed flashing with the next row of shakes. Cut notches in the shakes to fit around the stack, keeping a 1" gap between the stack and shakes.

(continued next page)

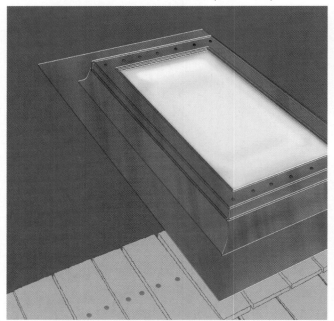

9 Install shakes under the bottom apron flashing beneath a skylight. Cut the shakes as necessary. Nail the shakes without driving nails through the flashing. Apply roofing cement to the underside of the flashing, then press to the shakes.

10 Interweave skylight flashing along the skylight with rows of shakes. After each row of shakes, install a piece of flashing with the vertical plane placed under the edge lip of the skylight and the horizontal plane flush with the bottom edge of the shake. A row of shakes covers the top apron flashing.

11 Apply roofing cement along the underside of the roof louver flange, then set it over the vent cutout and over the shakes directly below it. Nail the louver in place. Install shakes over the sides and back of the louver, trimming to fit, as needed.

12 As you approach the ridge, measure from the last installed row to the peak. Do this on each side of the roof. If the measurements are not equal, slightly adjust the exposure rate in successive rows until the measurements are the same. Make sure you're measuring to points that are aligned at the peak. The top of the sheathing is probably not level across the roof and cannot be a reference point.

13 Run shakes past the roof peak. Snap a chalk line across the shakes at the ridge. Set the circular saw blade to the depth of the shakes, then cut along the chalk line.

14 Cut 8" strips of felt paper and staple them over the hips and ridge. Set a factory-made hip and ridge cap at one end of the ridge, aligned with the roof peak. Do the same at the other end of the roof. Snap a chalk line between the outside edges of the caps.

Exposure rate

15 Set a ridge cap along the chalk line, flush with the edge of the roof, to serve as the starter. Install with two nails. Place a cap directly on top of the starter cap, and nail in place. Install caps along the remainder of the ridge, alternating the overlap pattern. The exposure rate should be the same as the roof shakes. Nails should penetrate the roof decking by ½".

Variation: If the ridge caps are not pre-assembled by the manufacturer, install the first cap along the chalk line, then place the second cap over the edge of the first. Alternate the overlap pattern across the ridge.

Roll roofing is used on roofs that have a slight slope. Installation is fast and straightforward, with the material rolled over a clean roof decking.

Installing Roll Roofing

Roll roofing is a quick and easy roofing product to install. The material is simply rolled across the roof, nailed along the edges, and sealed with roofing cement. It's geared for roofs with slight slopes, such as porches and garages.

Some manufacturers recommend priming the roof with a roof primer prior to installing the roofing. Read and follow manufacturer's directions. Your roof decking must be completely clean before the roll roofing can be applied. Any debris, even a small twig or leaf, can end up showing through the roofing.

Store the roofing in a warm, dry location until you're ready to start the project, and choose a warm day for the installation. Roll roofing is best installed in temperatures above 45°F. If applied in cold weather, the material can crack.

The following pages show the three methods for installing roll roofing. The exposed nail application, pages 87 to 88, is the fastest installation method and can be used on sloped roofs. The concealed nail application, page 89, is best for roofs with a slighter pitch, all the way down to a 1 in 12 slope, because it prevents water from penetrating under the nail heads. The double coverage method, also on page 89, is used for roofs that are almost completely flat. The double coverage, using selvage roofing, offers better protection against water infiltration.

Everything You Need

Tools: utility knife, tape measure, chalk line, serrated trowel, straightedge, hammer.

Materials: roll roofing, galvanized roofing nails, asphalt-based roofing cement.

How to Install Roll Roofing (Exposed Nail Application)

1 Nail drip edge along the eaves and rake ends of the roof (pages 64 to 65). Sweep the roof decking clean. Center an 18"-wide strip of roll roofing over the valley. Nail one side ¾" from the edge, every 6". Press the roofing firmly into the valley center, then nail the other side. Install a 36" strip over the valley the same way.

2 Snap a chalk line 35½" up from the eaves. Unroll the roofing along the chalk line, overhanging the eaves and rake edges by ½". Nail the roofing every 3" along the sides and bottom, ¾" from the edge of the decking. Roofing nails should be long enough to penetrate the roofing decking by at least ¾".

TIP: *Make sure the roofing is straight before nailing. Once it's nailed, you can't adjust it without creating wrinkles and folds. If it's running crooked, cut it and start with a new strip.*

3 Where more than one roll is needed to complete a course, apply roofing cement along the edge of the installed piece, using a trowel. Place a new roll 6" over the first piece. Press the seam together and drive nails every 3" along the end lap.

4 Apply 2" of roofing cement along the top edge of the installed course. Install the second row, flush with the line on the roofing, overlapping the cement edge. Drive nails every 3" along the rakes and overlap, ¾" from the edges. Do the same for remaining rows, offsetting seams at least 18".

(continued next page)

5 Cut roofing 1" from the valley center, using a utility knife and straightedge. Be careful not to cut into the valley roofing. Apply a 6" wide strip of roofing cement on the valley at the overlap. Place the main roofing over the cement. Nail in place every 3" along the seam.

6 Install roofing in front of a vent pipe. Cut a square of roofing to fit over the pipe, with a hole in the center. Apply roofing cement around the edges of the square, then set it in place over the pipe. Overlap with the next row of roofing, notching for the pipe as necessary.

TIP: *Use modest amounts of roofing cement. Excess cement can cause the roof to blister.*

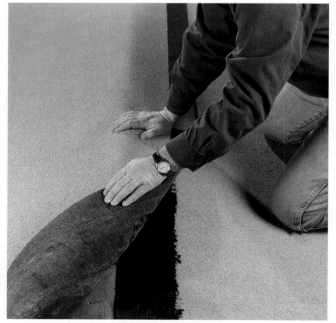

7 Cut the roofing flush with the roof peak. Snap a line on each side of the roof, 5½" from the peak. Apply 2" of cement above each line. Place a 12"-wide strip of roofing over the peak, flush with the chalk lines. Drive nails every 3" along the seams, ¾" from the edges.

Variation: Rather than install a strip over the ridge, extend the roofing on one side of the roof 6" past the peak, overlapping the opposite side. Nail along the edge to secure it to the decking. Do the same on the other side, overlapping the installed roofing at the peak. Apply cement along the seam, and nail in place.

How to Install Roll Roofing (Concealed Nail Application)

1 Cut 9"-wide strips of roofing. Nail them in place along the rakes and eaves. Snap a chalk line 35½" up from the eaves. Place the first course of roofing flush with the line.

2 Nail the roofing along the top edge only, driving nails every 4", ¾" from the top edge. Roll back the side and bottom edges. Apply cement along the outside 2" of the strips installed in step 1. Set the overlapping strip back in place, pressing firmly to seal.

3 Set the next course in place so it overlaps the first row by 4". Nail along the top edge. Lift the side and bottom edges, apply cement, then press together to seal. Repeat this process for the remainder of the roof.

How to Install Roll Roofing (Double Coverage Application)

1 Cut away the granule part of the roofing to create a starter strip. Align the strip with the eaves, and drive nails along the top and bottom edge at 12" intervals. Place the first full course flush with the eaves. Nail the non-granule edges every 12". Roll back the bottom of the roofing and apply roofing cement along the eaves and rake edges on the starter strips. Set the roofing back in place, pressing it into the cement.

2 Align the bottom edge of the second course with the top of the granule edge of the first row. Nail every 12" along the non-granule edges. Flip the bottom part back, apply cement along the sides and bottom of the non-granule area of the first course, then set the strip back in place. Install remaining courses the same way.

Metal roofs offer a sleek, stylish look that adds to the home's curb appeal. The roof looks similar to slate, but it's actually much lighter—and less expensive.

Installing Metal Roofing

Contrary to popular myth, metal roofs are not any more noisy than other types of roofs. A metal roofing system operates in much the same fashion as other roofing products—it uses a series of overlapping materials that dispel water. Unlike roofing materials in which each row overlays the previous row, metal roofs have an interlocking system so each panel overlaps and locks in place with adjacent panels or trim. This system keeps the roof watertight and helps hold the materials in place.

The installation techniques for metal roofing vary by material and manufacturer. The steel roof shown on pages 92 to 95 features panels that mimic the look of slate. The panels have lips on all four sides that interlock with other panels and trim pieces. Each panel is fastened to the roof with clips that also lock on the panels' lips. The trim is pre-formed for easy installation and to allow panels and trim to conveniently interlock. For an overview of how the components fit together, see the detail drawings on the opposite page.

A different type of steel roofing is also shown on the opposite page. These panels interlock along the top and bottom lips, but the sides form an overlap by each panel sliding over the edges of the preceding panel. The panels are installed with screws, rather than with clips.

Another popular type of metal roofing—vertical roofing—is shown on pages 96 to 97. This roofing also uses an interlocking system, although the panels are installed vertically rather than horizontally. Detail drawings on the opposite page show how the panels and trim fit together. To simplify the installation process, most manufacturers will size the panels to fit your roof. If you give the manufacturer the dimensions of your roof, you can get panels that span the length of your roof.

Before choosing a metal roofing, read manufacturer's recommendations for roofing requirements. Some products require a specific roof pitch, such as a minimum of a 15° slope. During installation, try to avoid walking on panels as much as possible. When it's necessary, walk on the flat part of the panels, not the locks or channels.

Everything You Need

Metal Roof

Tools: hammer, tape measure, cordless drill, hemming tool, aviation snips, pop rivet gun, caulk gun.

Materials: metal roofing system, ice and water shield, 30# felt paper, #10 pancake head wood screws, #8 truss head screws, tape sealant, $\frac{1}{8} \times \frac{3}{16}$" rivets, tube sealant.

Vertical Metal Roof

Tools: hammer, tape measure, tin snips, caulk gun, utility knife, locking sheet-metal tool, cordless drill.

Materials: metal roofing, 12-gauge galvanized roofing nails with $\frac{3}{8}$" heads, caulk, roofing manufacturer's paint, ice and water shield, 30# felt paper, trim coil, silicone sealant, stainless steel screws.

Anatomy of Metal Roofing Installation

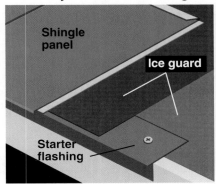

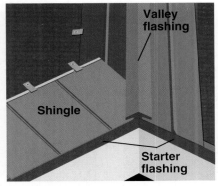

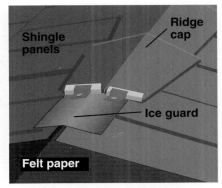

Ice guard is placed under and then over the starter flashing. The first row of shingles interlocks with the starter flashing.

Valley flashing fits over the valley, and the front edge overlaps the starter flashing. Shingles are cut to fit along the valley.

Strips of ice guard are set over the ridge, covering the tops of the last rows of shingles. Ridge caps are installed over the ice guard.

Variation for Installing Metal Roofing

1 Following the manufacturer's recommended offset, install the shingles one row at a time. Overlap shingles so the top panel clicks into the lock of the underlying panel.

2 Keep the top edges of adjacent panels flush. Slide panels together so the gap between the top clip-locks is no more than ³⁄₁₆".

3 Drive a number 8 hex head, corrosion-resistant screw through the upper left corner of the shingle. Drive a screw in the top right-hand corner, and two screws in between the corners.

Anatomy of Vertical Metal Roofing Installation

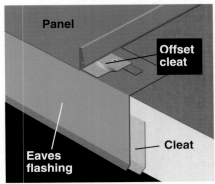

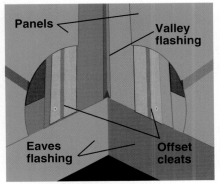

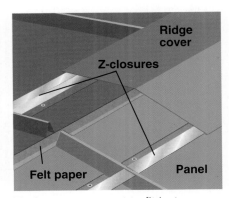

A cleat is fastened to the fascia, then the eaves flashing is installed over the cleat. An offset cleat is placed over the eaves flashing to interlock with the lip of the panels.

Valley flashing is set over the valley, overlapping the eaves flashing. Offset cleats are installed along the valley flashing. Panels are cut to fit along the valley, and interlock with the offset cleats.

Z-closures are cut to fit between the ribs of the panels. Once they're installed, the ridge cover is placed over the z-closures and both sides of the roof.

1 Cover the roof with ice guard and felt paper (pages 62 to 63), then place the starter flashing tight against the fascia. Nail the starter strip to the roof deck and fascia every 18". Overlap starter strips by 2" if more than one is needed. Place a layer of ice and water shield over the starter strip.

2 Cut a ¾" notch in the locking lip at the bottom of the first gable trim flashing, 1¼" from the outside edge, to create a weep hole. Set the gable flashing tight against the rake, overlapping the starter flashing. Fasten the gable flashing in place by attaching a clip and nailing it to the roof decking every 18" and face nailing through the drip edge at 18" intervals.

3 Where more than one gable trim flashing is needed, cut 1½" notch from the bottom of the channel of the overlapping piece, then overlap the trim flashings 1½".

4 Center the valley pan over the valley and cut to fit so the end slightly overlaps the starter flashing. Fasten the valley pan to the decking with clips every 18". Fold the end of the valley pan over the starter flashing, using a locking sheet-metal tool.

5 To overlap valley pans, cut the locking lips 1½" from the bottom edge on the overlapping piece. Apply sealant to the end of the first valley pan, then overlap it 1½" with the second piece. Fasten a clip over both valley pans at the seam.

6 Cut a 2" notch for a weep hole in the lip at the bottom left corner of the first shingle. Place the shingle in the bottom left corner of the roof. Interlock the outside edge with the gable trim, and tightly lock the bottom lip to the starter flashing. Fasten to the decking with a minimum of three clips.

TIP: *Install shingles from left to right, with a minimum of three clips per shingle.*

7 Cut a 2" weep hole in the second shingle and set it in place so it interlocks with both the first shingle and the starter flashing. Fasten with clips. Install the remaining shingles in the first course the same way, interlocking the edges. Note: Remaining courses of shingles do not have weep holes.

8 To begin the second row, cut a shingle at the number 2 marked at the top of the panel. Install the cut shingle. Complete the second course, then move on to the next rows, cutting the first shingle in row three at the number 3 marked on the panel, and at the number 4 for the fourth panel. On the fifth row, start over with a full shingle.

(continued next page)

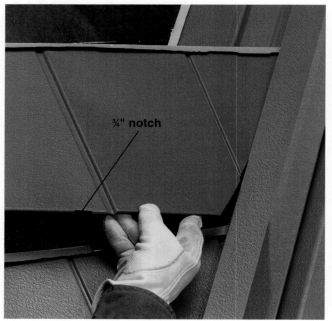

9 Cut panels to fit against the valley flashing. Cut a ¾" notch for a weep hole in the bottom lip of each shingle that abuts the valley. Keep the notch 6" from the center of valley, making sure it falls within the valley pan. Do this for each row of shingles along the valley, except the first row.

10 If your roof has a dormer, install shingles as close to the front of the dormer as possible. Cut and bend trim coil to fit under the siding or flashing and overlap the last row of shingles. Nail the flashing to the dormer and caulk the nail heads.

11 To complete the dormer, place the sidewall flashing against the dormer, overlapping the trim coil installed in step 10. If the dormer is sided, slide the flashing under the siding. Nail to the dormer. Cut shingles to fit in the sidewall flashing.

12 Cut shingles to fit snugly around pipes. Install a panel over the pipe, folding back the top locking edge on the shingle above the pipe where the flashing will sit. Place the pipe flashing over the pipe and fasten with screws that are long enough to penetrate the roof decking. Caulk around the flashing. Set the next row of shingles over the flashing.

13 Cut shingles to match the roof holes for each louver. Install the shingles over the holes. Fold back the top lock on the shingle where the louver will sit. Install the roof louver over the shingles, fasten with screws that penetrate the roof decking, and caulk around the louver flashing. Place the next row of shingles over the back edge of the louver flashing.

14 Cut shingles flush with hips and ridges. Cut 4"-wide strips of ice guard and place them over hips and ridges. Set the first ridge cap over the ice guard at one end of the roof, overlapping the gable flashing. Face nail the ridge cap in place, then caulk the nail heads.

15 Fasten the remaining ridge caps in place using clips. Face nail the last ridge cap and caulk the heads. Install ridge caps on remaining hips and ridges the same way.

16 Using the paint supplied by the manufacturer, touch up any shingles that have been scratched.

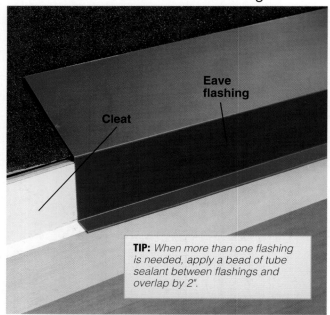

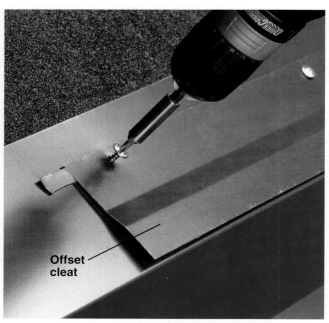

1 Cover the roof with ice guard and felt paper (pages 62 to 63). Fasten a cleat to the fascia at a height that will allow the eave flashing to lie flat on the roof. Drive pancake head wood screws every 12". Slide the hem of the eave flashing over the cleat and fasten with wood screws through the top edge every 48".

TIP: *When more than one flashing is needed, apply a bead of tube sealant between flashings and overlap by 2".*

2 Apply tape sealant along the underside top edge of the offset cleat. Place the cleat over the top of the eave flashing so the outer edges are aligned. Fasten the cleat with wood screws driven through the tape sealant every 12".

3 Center the valley flashing over the valley and tack it in place with screws every 48". Fasten tape sealant along both sides of the valley, 5" from the center.

4 Align offset cleats 3" from the valley center. Fasten in place with screws every 12". Drive the screws through the tape on the valley flashing.

5 Cut a 1½" notch in the end of the ribs of the first roofing panel. Bend the flat part of the panel back 180° to create a hem, using a hemming tool. Apply sealant in the panel hem.

6 Set the panel over the offset cleat, starting at the rake edge. Square the panel to the eave flashing. Drive truss head screws in the center of the fastening groove on the panel's male (right) side.

7 Notch and hem the second panel, following step 5. Apply sealant in the hem. Snap the second panel over the first and place against the offset cleat. Fasten in place with screws. Install remaining panels the same way.

8 Cut panels parallel to the valley, using aviation snips. Notch and hem panels to fit the offset cleats along the valley, using the hemming tool. Fill the hem with a bead of sealant, then install over the offset cleat.

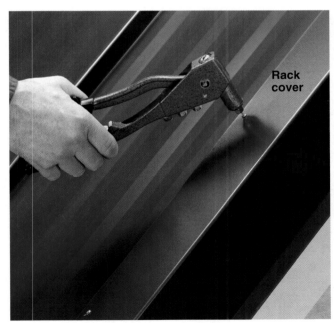

Rack cover

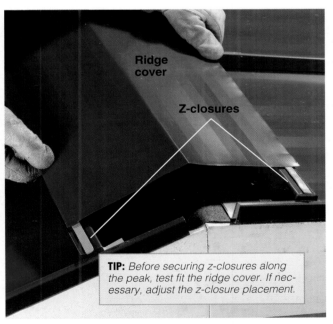

Ridge cover

Z-closures

TIP: *Before securing z-closures along the peak, test fit the ridge cover. If necessary, adjust the z-closure placement.*

9 Place tape sealant next to the rib along the rake end. Set a z-closure over the tape and install with wood screws every 12". Place tape sealant over the top leg of the z-closure. Fasten a cleat to the rake of the house at a height that allows the rake cover to fit over the cleat and lie flat over the z-closure. Slide the rack cover over the cleat and fasten to the z-closure, using a rivet gun with pop rivets every 12".

10 Place a row of tape sealant across the panels and ribs, 4" from the top edge. Cut z-closures 2" longer than panel widths, then cut the top and bottom legs 1" from the edge. Cut off the top legs 1" from each end, then fold the ends back. Install z-closures on the tape between ribs, using four screws each. Place tape sealant over the z-closures. Set the ridge cover over the z-closures and install with pop rivets.

Installing Tile Roofing

Modern clay tiles use an "S" type design rather than the two-piece system that was once common. This simplifies the installation process and saves you time. Due to the contour of the tiles, you'll need plumbing vents and air vents that match the shape of the roofing materials. See the reference list on page 248 for manufacturer information.

Before starting the project, make sure your roof framing can support the weight of the tiles. The materials are very heavy, and roofs designed for asphalt shingles may not have the structural support for clay tile. Check with your building inspector if you're unsure.

Everything You Need

Tools: hammer, tape measure, chalk line, circular saw, jig saw, trowel, diamond saw blade, caulk gun.

Materials: 30# felt paper, ice and water shield, 2 × 6 nailers, 2 × 3 nailers, 2 × 2 nailers, corrosion-resistant 11 gauge nails, roofing nails, sand, portland cement, plastic cement, cement mortar Type M, tile, bird stops, plumbing vents, air vents, roofing sealant, peel-and-stick flashing, plastic cement.

Photo courtesy of M.C.A. Superior Clay Roof Tile

Tips for Installing a Tile Roof

To cut clay tile, use a diamond blade in a circular saw or grinder. Clamp the tile to a worksurface, make your cutting line on the tile, then cut along the line. Be sure to wear safety glasses and a respirator when making the cuts.

Mortar is available premixed, or you can mix it yourself. This project requires cement mortar Type M. To mix it, combine 3 parts portland cement, 1 part lime, and 12 parts sand. Add water and mix until the consistency is like mashed potatoes.

Clay tiles give homes a truly impressive roof that can't be imitated by other materials. The "S" design makes installation easier and less time consuming. Each tile simply overlaps the preceding tile (inset).

How to Install a Tile Roof

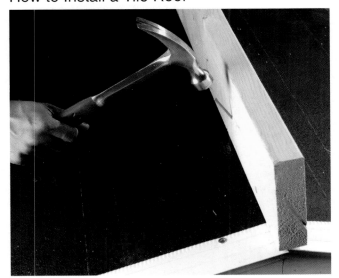

1 Cover the roof with underlayment (pages 62 to 63). Install drip edge (pages 64 to 65) and valley flashing (pages 66 to 67). Nail 2 × 6 lumber on edge over all ridges and hips.

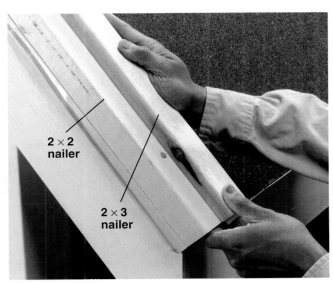

2 Install 2 × 2 nailers along the rake edges of the roof. Butt 2 × 3 nailers against the 2 × 2s and nail them in place.

(continued next page)

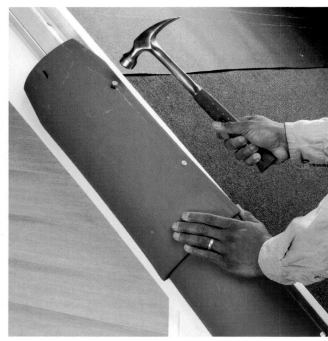

3 Measuring from the outside edge of the 2 × 3 nailer along the left rake edge, make marks on the roof every 12". Center a bird stop over each mark, aligned with the front edge of the roof, and nail in place. Note: bird stops are available from the tile manufacturer, or you can cut your own from wood.

4 Place gable tile over the 2 × 2s along the rake ends of the roof, overhanging the front of the roof by 3". Nail in place, using two 11 gauge nails per tile. Overlap tiles by 3". Note: Be sure to use left gable tiles for the left side and right gable tiles for the right side.

TIP: To ensure alignment, tie a string across the end of the first gable tiles. Set the tiles flush with the string. Move the string to align subsequent rows.

5 Starting on the left side of the roof, place the first field tile over the gable tile and 2 × 3 nailer. Align the end of the field tile with the end of the gable tile. Nail in place with two nails. Install the first course of tiles the same way, placing them over the bird stops.

6 Install the next row of tiles on the roof, overlapping the first course by 3". Install remaining courses the same way.

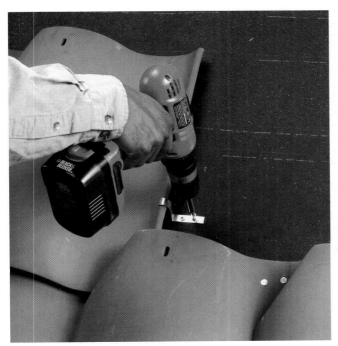

Option: In areas subject to high winds, install 2½" stainless steel hurricane clips. Install the clip on the side lap of the tile, near the front edge. Fasten to the roof deck with a 1½" screw. Use one clip per tile.

7 Cut tile parallel to the center of the valley flashing. Tiles should overlap the edges of the flashing by at least 4".

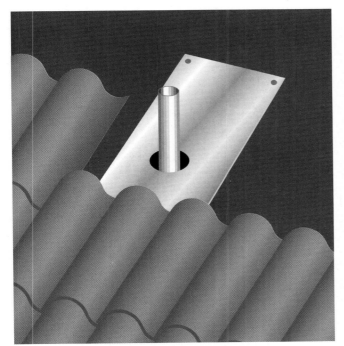

8 Place primary metal flashing over a plumbing vent and nail in the corners. Install tile over the front of the flashing.

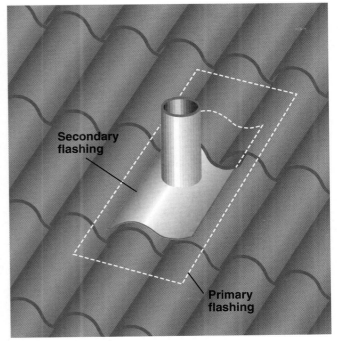

Secondary flashing

Primary flashing

9 Cover the back edge of the flashing with felt paper. Install tile over the flashing and vent. Apply roofing sealant along the underside of the secondary flashing, then place it over the tiles and vent. Overlap the back edge of the flashing with the next row of tiles.

(continued next page)

10 At dormers, chimneys, and walls, install pan flashing at least 4" up the wall and a minimum of 6" along the roof. Turn up the outside edge of the flashing 1½". Install counterflashing over the pan flashing. Note: The top edge of the counterflashing must be installed under the wall siding or placed in the mortar between bricks in the chimney. The flashing may still be present from the old roof.

11 Install a 2 × 3 nailer along the turned-up edge of the pan flashing. Set the tile over the nailer and nail it in place.

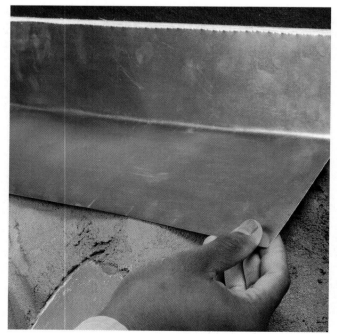

12 When the roofing abuts a wall of the house, install tile up the roof to the wall. Apply cement mortar generously between the tops of the tiles and the wall, filling in any gaps. Place 3 × 4 flashing over the mortar, then place counterflashing over that.

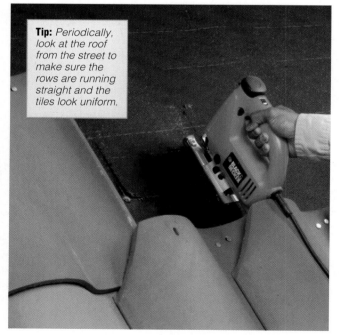

Tip: Periodically, look at the roof from the street to make sure the rows are running straight and the tiles look uniform.

13 Mark roof vent locations between rows of tiles and between rafters. Follow manufacturer's guidelines for the size of the opening. Cut out the opening, using a jig saw or circular saw.

14 Apply roofing sealant along the bottom of the primary roof vent, then install it over the opening, using roofing nails driven every 4" through the flange. Seal the flange with peel-and-stick flashing. Place the secondary vent over the primary vent and nail it to the roof. Overlap the lip with the next piece of tile.

15 Mix cement mortar Type M and apply it around the nailers at the hips and peak. Also apply mortar over the tops and in between tiles abutting the nailers.

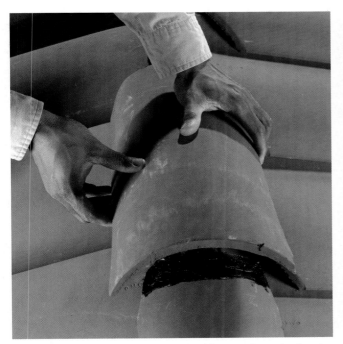

16 Center ridge tiles over the hips and peak. Apply a small amount of plastic cement on the nose of each ridge tile. Overlap the tiles for a 16" exposure, placing the tile over the plastic cement on the previous tile. Nail the ridge tiles, using two nails per tile.

17 Mix one part Type 1 portland cement with three parts sand, add water sparingly for a thick consistency, to create a rich cement mortar. Apply the mortar along the exposed edges of the hip and ridge tiles.

Siding Installation

The siding protects the house against wind, rain, snow, sun, and other forces of nature. To successfully perform these tasks, the siding must be watertight and securely fastened in place.

Each type of siding typically has its own unique installation process, and each application requires the correct underlayment, fasteners, and nailing method. Siding installation can even vary between manufacturers' products. For example, vinyl shakes tend to have different nailing patterns and different locking mechanisms, depending on the manufacturer.

The projects in this section detail general installation of siding materials, but you may need to modify the instructions slightly to fit your particular project. Before jumping into the siding job, familiarize yourself with the entire installation process so you know what's in store. If you're also planning to install new soffits, complete the soffit project before starting on the siding (see page 175).

Without exception, the jobs will be much easier and can be completed quicker if you have a helper. This is especially true of siding materials that are difficult to manage by yourself, such as wood lap siding and log cabin siding. Having an assistant hand you materials also saves you trips up and down the ladder.

Siding your own house is one of the most gratifying home improvement projects. Your hard work will be highly visible to your neighbors and guests, and you'll feel a sense of accomplishment every time you look at your house.

Types of Siding

The goal of any siding installation is to end up with a great-looking finish. The applications used to get there are as varied as the sidings themselves.

Siding is typically installed with each row overlapping the underlying row. For lap siding, the top piece rests over the top of the piece below. For vinyl, the overlapping piece snaps together with the preceding row. With brick, each row is placed directly on top of the underlying course.

Be sure you understand the application techniques for the type of siding you're installing, and be sure to use the recommended fasteners.

Combining two types of siding can enhance the curb appeal of your home. This house features stone and fiber cement siding.

Photo courtesy of James Hardie® Siding Products

Lap siding features panels in an overlapping pattern that create crisp, horizontal lines. The look has been a traditional favorite for homeowners. The panels are usually wood, fiber cement, or vinyl.

Photo courtesy of James Hardie® Siding Products

Shakes and shingles closely resemble each other, although shingles are thinner and smaller than shakes. Most authentic shakes and shingles are made of Western cedar.

Photo courtesy of Rocky Mountain Log Homes

Log cabin siding offers a rustic, rural look that has a broad appeal. Actual logs are used on some homes, while others use siding that mimics the look of log cabins.

Photo courtesy of James Hardie® Siding Products

Vertical siding can make homes appear taller by drawing the eye skyward. Board and batten is a popular vertical siding, and some vinyl sidings can also be installed vertically.

Photo courtesy of Vande Hey Raleigh

Brick siding is a durable exterior that doesn't require a lot of maintenance. Bricks are made of fired clay, and are available in a variety of colors, textures, and shapes.

Photo courtesy of La Habra Stucco

Stucco siding has an aesthetic appeal all its own. Because it's not installed in rows, it's one of the few sidings that doesn't have horizontal or vertical lines running through it.

Tools & Materials for Siding

Basic construction and remodeling tools are all you need for wood, fiber cement, and vinyl siding projects. If you don't have some of these cutting, measuring, or leveling tools, it's worthwhile to buy them. They're not very expensive, and you'll get a lot of use out of them for other common home improvement and repair projects.

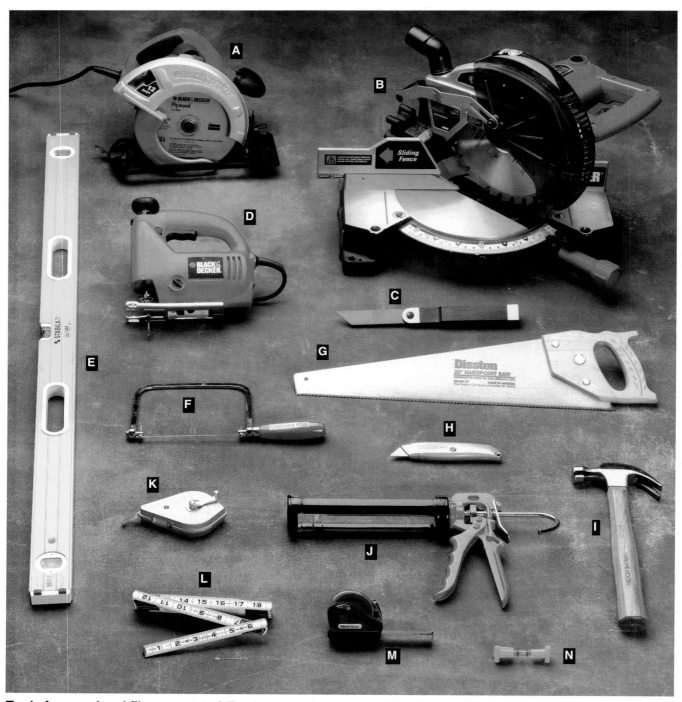

Tools for wood and fiber cement siding include: circular saw (A), miter saw (B), T-bevel (C), jig saw (D), level (E), coping saw (F), handsaw (G), utility knife (H), hammer (I), caulk gun (J), chalk line (K), folding tape measure (L), tape measure (M), and line level (N).

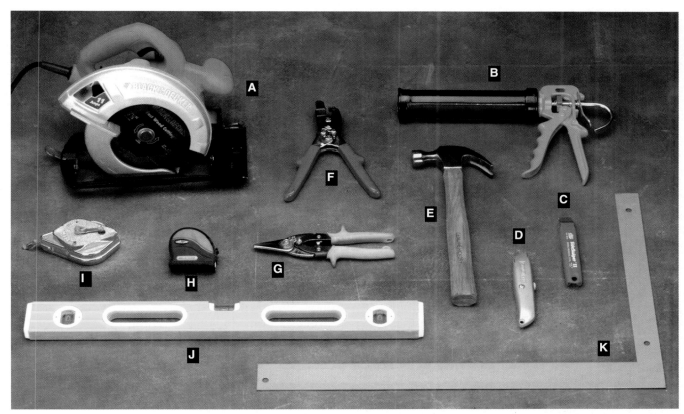

Tools for vinyl siding include: circular saw (A), caulk gun (B), zip tool (C), utility knife (D), hammer (E), nail slot punch (F), aviation snips (G), tape measure (H), chalk line (I), level (J), and framing square (K).

Caulks for siding include (from left): concrete and masonry silicone caulk, concrete sealant, acrylic latex caulk, acrylic latex caulk with silicone, and latex sealant.

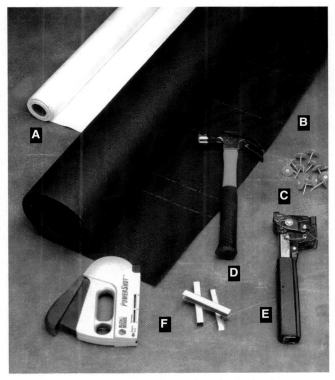

Underlayment materials for siding include: housewrap (A), felt paper (B), cap nails (C), hammer (D), hammer stapler (E), and staple gun and staples (F).

Removing Exterior Siding

Although it's sometimes possible to install new siding over old if the old siding is solid and firmly attached to the house, it's often better to remove the siding, especially if it's damaged. Taking off the old siding allows you to start with a flat, smooth surface. And because the overall thickness of the siding will remain unchanged, you won't have to add extensions to your window and door jambs.

There's no "right" way to remove siding. Each type of siding material is installed differently, and consequently, they have different removal techniques. A couple of universal rules do apply, however. Start by removing trim that's placed over the siding, and work from the top down. Siding is usually installed from the bottom up, and working in the opposite direction makes removal much easier. Determine the best removal method for your project based on your type of siding.

Strip one side of the house at a time, then re-side that wall before ripping the siding off another section. This minimizes the amount of time your bare walls are exposed to the elements. Take care not to damage the sheathing. If you can't avoid tearing the housewrap, it can easily be replaced, but the sheathing is another story.

While the goal is to remove the siding as quickly as possible, it's also important to work safely. Take care when working around windows so the siding doesn't crack or break the glass. Invest the necessary time to protect the flowers and shrubs before starting the tear-off (pages 44 to 45).

Renting a dumpster will expedite the cleanup process. It's much easier to dispose of the siding as soon as it's removed rather than stacking it up in an unsightly pile in your yard, then throwing it away later. When you're finished with your cleanup, use a release magnet to collect the nails on the ground.

Everything You Need

Tools: cat's paw, flat pry bar, zip tool, drill, circular saw, masonry chisel, hammer, masonry-cutting blade, masonry bit, aviation snips, roofing shovel, release magnet.

The exterior wall is composed of siding, housewrap or felt paper, and sheathing. Remove the siding without disturbing or damaging the sheathing.

Sheathing

Felt paper

Insulation

Siding

Tips for Removing Siding

Brick molding comes preattached to most wood-frame window and door units. To remove the molding, pry along the outside of the frame to avoid marring the exposed parts of the jambs and molding.

Lap siding is nailed at the top, then covered by the next course. Pry off the trim at the top of the wall to expose the nails in top row. Remove the nails using a cat's paw, and work your way down the wall.

Shakes and shingles are best removed with a roofing shovel. Use the shovel to pry the siding away from the wall. Once the siding is removed, use the shovel or a hammer to pull out remaining nails.

Board and batten siding is removed by prying off the battens from over the boards. Use a pry bar or cat's paw to remove the nails from the boards.

Siding shown cutaway for clarity

Vinyl siding has a locking channel that fits over the nailing strip of the underlying piece. To remove, use a zip tool to separate the panels, and use a flat pry bar or hammer to remove the nails.

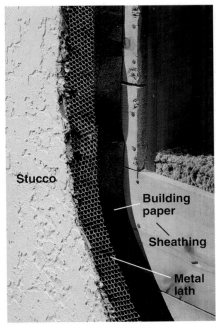

Stucco

Building paper

Sheathing

Metal lath

Stucco siding is difficult to remove. It's usually much easier to apply the new siding over the stucco than to remove it. If you're determined to take it off, use a cold chisel and hammer to break it into pieces, and aviation snips to cut the lath.

Although the sheathing isn't visible, a smooth, solid sheathing installation is essential to a professional looking siding finish.

Replacing Wall Sheathing

After removing the old siding, inspect the sheathing to make sure it's still in good condition. If water penetrated behind the siding, there's a good chance the sheathing is warped, rotted, or otherwise damaged, and will need to be replaced. You'll only need to replace the section of sheathing that's damaged. Before cutting into the wall, make sure there are no wires, cables, or pipes under the sheathing.

Older homes typically have planks or plywood sheathing, while new homes may have a

nonstructural sheathing. The replacement material doesn't have to be the same material as the original sheathing, but it does have to be the same thickness.

Everything You Need

Tools: hammer, circular saw, tape measure, chalk line, pry bar.

Materials: sheathing, 2 x 4, 3" deck screws, 2¼" deck screws, drill.

How to Replace Wall Sheathing

1 Snap chalk lines around the area of damaged sheathing, making sure the vertical lines are next to wall studs. Remove any nails or staples in your path. Set the depth of the circular saw blade to cut through the sheathing, but not cut the studs.

2 Pry off the damaged sheathing. Remove any remaining nails or staples in the studs. Measure the opening, subtract ⅛" from each side, then cut a piece of sheathing to size.

3 Align 2 × 4 nailing strips with the edges of the wall studs. Fasten the strips in place, using 3" deck screws.

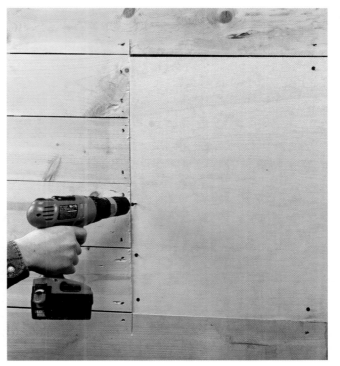

4 Place the new piece of sheathing in the opening, keeping a ⅛" gap on each side to allow for expansion. Attach the sheathing to the nailing strips and studs, using 2¼" deck screws driven every 12".

Installing Housewrap

Housewrap is a specially engineered fabric that blocks air and water infiltration from the outside, but allows moisture vapor to pass through from the inside. It's best to apply the housewrap before installing windows and doors, but since that's not always possible with a remodeling or siding replacement job, you can cut the housewrap to fit around them.

When installing, make sure the stud marks on the housewrap are aligned with the wall studs. Most siding materials need to be nailed to studs, and the marks on the housewrap identify their locations. Staples are permissible for fastening housewrap, but cap nails are recommended and have better holding power.

Felt paper is not the same as housewrap. It's not necessarily designed to work as an air barrier, and it may absorb water. Do not substitute felt paper when housewrap is supposed to be used.

**Housewrap helps protect
the house** from its worst enemies—water, moisture, and air infiltration. Covering exterior walls with housewrap before installing siding can also reduce your energy bills.

Everything You Need

Tools: hammer, utility knife, tape dispenser.

Materials: housewrap, cap nails, 2" or 3" contractor tape.

How to Install Housewrap

1 Starting 6" to 12" around a corner and 3" over the foundation to cover the sill plate, unroll the housewrap along the side of the house with the printed side facing out. Align the printed stud marks on the housewrap with the stud marks on the sheathing. Keep the roll straight as you unwrap it.

2 Nail the housewrap every 12" to 18" on the vertical stud lines, using cap nails. Keep the housewrap pulled snug as it's unrolled. Cut holes in the housewrap for extrusions, such as hose spigots and the electric meter.

3 When starting a new roll, overlap vertical seams by 6" to 12", aligning the stud marks. Begin the second course by overlapping the bottom course 6". Once again, make sure stud marks are lined up.

4 At window and door locations, cut the housewrap at the middle of the nailing flanges. At the bottom, cut the housewrap at the sill. Pull the sill and jamb flashing over the housewrap. Be careful not to slice the nailing flanges and windowsills when cutting the housewrap.

5 Tape all horizontal and vertical seams, accidental tears, and seams around doors, windows, and plumbing and electrical protrusions, using contractor tape. Tape the bottom of the protrusion first, then the sides, then place a piece of tape over the top.

Vinyl siding can look very similar to wood lap siding, but it doesn't require regular upkeep. Vinyl can be installed on any type and style of house.

Installing Vinyl Siding

Vinyl has become one of the most popular sidings due to its low cost, uniform appearance, and maintenance-free durability. Installation is fairly simple, with each row locking onto the lip of the underlying course, then nailed along the top.

There are a couple of key factors that will make or break your siding project. First, the sheathing must be straight and solid before the siding is applied. The siding will only look as straight and smooth as the wall it's on. Second, determine how the siding should overlap to hide the seams from the main traffic patterns. This usually means starting in the back and working toward the front of the house.

Do not nail the siding tight to the house. The panels need to slide back and forth as they expand and contract with changes in the temperature. If the siding can't move, it will bow, and will need to be reinstalled. Keep a 1/32" gap between the head of the nail and the siding.

Vinyl siding is available in a wide variety of colors and styles, and with a lot of accessories, such as trim, fluted lineals, vertical columns, crown molding, and band boards. The most common vinyl siding is horizontal lap siding, which is shown starting on page 118. This project shows using a foam underlayment, which reduces outside noise, protects the siding from dents, and adds an insulation value. Vertical vinyl siding is also available. It's specifically made for vertical applications. Pages 124 to 125 show how this type of vinyl siding is installed. Vinyl shakes are another type of vinyl siding, and that installation is shown on pages 126 to 127.

Everything You Need

Tools: hammer, circular saw or radial-arm saw, clamps, tape measure, string, straightedge, utility knife, aviation snips, level, chalk line, framing square, nail slot punch, zip-lock tool, snaplock punch, caulk gun.

Materials: vinyl siding, J-channel, corner posts, undersill, starter strip, nails, cutting table, safety glasses, silicone caulk.

Tips for Cutting Vinyl Siding

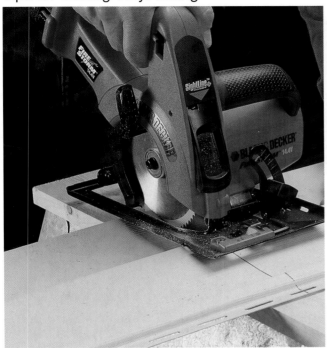

Use a fine-tooth blade installed backward in the saw to cut vinyl siding. Use a radial-arm saw or a circular saw, and move the blade slowly through the siding. Always wear safety glasses when cutting siding.

Support the siding on a cutting table when cutting. Vinyl siding is too flimsy to be placed across sawhorses without support. You can build a cutting table by fastening a long piece of scrap plywood between two sawhorses.

Tips for Using Specialty Tools

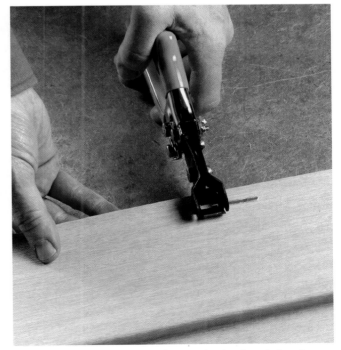

A snaplock punch is used to make raised tabs, or dimples, in a cut edge of siding where the nailing helm has been removed. This eliminates the need to face nail the panel.

A nail slot punch is used to make horizontal nail slots in the face of panels. It can also be used to add or elongate the opening of an existing nail slot to match irregular stud spacing.

How to Install Vinyl Siding

1 Install housewrap following instructions on pages 114 to 115. Identify the lowest corner of the house that has sheathing, and partially drive a nail 1½" above the bottom edge of the sheathing. Run a level string to the opposite corner of the wall and partially drive a nail. Do this around the entire house. Snap chalk lines between the nails.

2 Place the top edge of the starter strip along the chalk line and nail every 10". Nail in the center of the slots and don't nail tight to the house. Keep a ¼" gap between strips, and leave space at the corners for a ½" gap between starter strips and corner posts.

Option: Install vinyl siding underlayment on the house, using cap nails. Align the bottom of the underlayment with the starting strip. To cut panels to size, score them with a utility knife, then break them over your cutting table. Some panels need to be taped at the seams. Follow manufacturer's recommendations.

3 Install a corner post, keeping a ¼" gap between the top of the post and the soffit. Extend the bottom of the post ¼" below the bottom of the starter strip. Drive a nail at the top end of the uppermost slot on each side of the post (the post hangs from these nails). Make sure the post is plumb on both sides, using a level. Secure the post by driving nails every 8" to 12" in the center of the slots. Do not nail the post tight. Install the other posts the same way.

4 If more than one corner post is needed to span the length of a corner, the upper post overlaps the lower post. For an outside corner post, cut off 1" from the nailing flanges on the bottom edge of the top post. For an inside corner post, cut off 1" from the nailing flange on the upper edge of the bottom post. Overlap the posts by ¾", leaving ¼" for expansion.

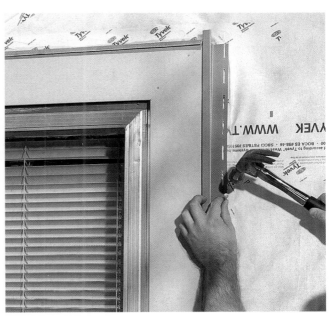

5 Measure and cut two J-channels that are the length of a window plus the width of the J-channel. Place one of the J-channels against the side of the window, aligning the bottom edge with the bottom edge of the window. Nail the channel in place. Nail the second J-channel against the opposite side of the window the same way.

6 At the top of the window, measure between the outside edges of the side J-channels and cut a piece of J-channel to fit. Cut a ¾" tab at each end. Bend the tabs down to form a drip edge. Miter cut the face at each end at 45°. Center the J-channel over the window and nail it in place. The top J-channel overlaps the side pieces, and the drip edges fit inside the side pieces. Do this for each window and door.

7 Measure, cut, and install J-channel along the gable ends. Nail the channels every 8" to 12". To overlap J-channels, cut 1" from the nailing hem. Overlap the channels ¾", leaving ¼" for expansion. At the gable peak, cut one channel at an angle to butt against the peak. Miter the channel on the opposite side to overlap the first channel.

(continued next page)

8 To install J-channel over a roof line, snap a chalk line along the roof flashing, ½" above the roof. Align the bottom edge of the J-channel along the chalk line, and nail the channel in place. Make sure the channel does not make direct contact with the shingles.

9 Measure, cut, and install undersill beneath each window. The undersill should be flush with the outside lip of the side channels.

10 Measure, cut, and install undersill along the horizontal eaves on the house. If more than one undersill is needed, cut the nailing hem 1¼" from the end of one undersill. Overlap the undersills by 1".

11 Snap the locking leg on the bottom of the first panel onto the starter strip, making sure it's securely locked in place. Keep a ¼" gap between the end of the panel and the corner post. Nail the panel a minimum of every 16" on center. Don't drive the nails tight. Note: This installation shows a vinyl siding underlayment in place.

12 Overlap panels by 1". Cut panels so the factory cut edge is the one that's visible. Keep nails at least 6" from the end of panels to allow for smooth overlap. Do not overlap panels directly under a window.

13 Place the second row over the first, snapping the locking leg into the lock of the underlying panels. Leave ¼" gap at corners and J-channels. Install subsequent rows, staggering seams at least 24" unless separated by more than three rows. Check every several rows for level. Make adjustments in slight increments, if necessary.

14 For hose spigots, pipes, and other protrusions, create a seam at the obstacle. Begin with a new panel to avoid extra seams. Cut an opening ¼" larger than the obstacle, planning for a 1" overlap of siding. Match the shape and contour as closely as possible. Fit the panels together around the obstruction and nail in place.

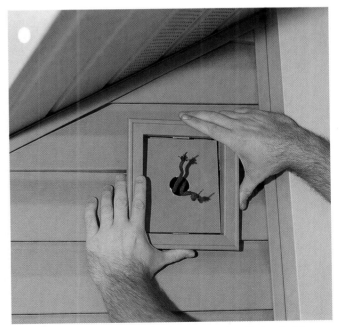

15 Place mounting blocks around outlets, lights, and doorbells. Assemble the base around the fixture, making sure it's level, and nail in place. Install siding panels, cutting them to fit around the mounting block with a ¼" gap on each side. Fasten the cover by snapping it over the block.

(continued next page)

16 Where panels must be notched to fit below a window, position the panel below the window and mark the edges of the window, allowing for a ¼" gap. Place a scrap piece of siding alongside the window and mark the depth of the notch, keeping a ¼" gap. Transfer the measurement to the panel, mark the notch, and cut it out. Create tabs on the outside face every 6", using a snap lock punch. Install the panel, locking the tabs into the undersill.

17 Install cut panels between windows and between windows and corners as you would regular panels. Avoid overlapping panels and creating seams in small spaces. The panels need to align with panels on the opposite side of the window.

18 To fit siding over a window, hold the panel in place over the window and mark it. Use a scrap piece of siding to mark the depth of the cut. Transfer the measurement to the full panel and cut the opening. Fit the cut edge into the J-channel above the window, lock the panel in place, and nail it.

19 For dormers, measure up from the bottom of the J-channel the height of a panel and make a mark. Measure across to the opposite J-channel. Use this measurement to mark and cut the panel to size. Cut and install panels for the rest of the dormer the same way.

20 Measure the distance between the lock on the last fully installed panel and the top of the undersill under the horizontal eaves. Subtract ¼", then mark and rip a panel to fit. Use a snaplock punch to punch tabs on the outside face every 6". Install the panel, locking the tabs into the undersill.

21 Place a scrap panel in the J-channel along the gable end of the house. Place another scrap over the last row of panels before the gable starts, slide it under the first scrap, and mark the angle where they intersect. Transfer this angle to full panels. Make a similar template for the other side. Cut the panels and set the cut edge into the J-channel, leaving a ¼" gap.

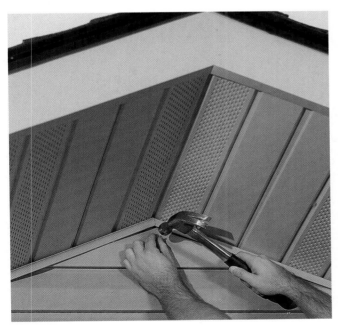

22 Cut the last piece of siding to fit the gable peak. Drive a single aluminum or stainless steel finish nail through the top of the panel to hold it in place. This is the only place where you will face nail the siding.

23 Apply caulk between all windows and J-channel, and between doors and J-channel.

How to Install Vertical Vinyl Siding

1 Cover the walls with housewrap (see pages 114 to 115). Snap a level chalk line around the base of each wall where the siding will start. Install corner posts, following step 3 on page 118. Install J-channel around doors and windows, following steps 5 to 6 on page 119. Note: Under windows, use J-channel rather than undersill.

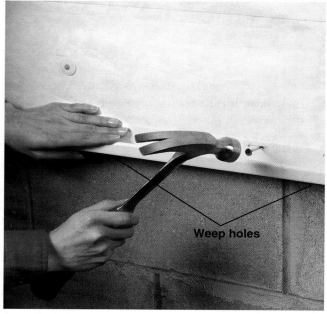

Weep holes

2 Drill ¼" weep holes in J-channel every 24". Align the bottom edge of this J-channel, which serves as starter strip, with the chalk line. Drive nails in the center of the slots every 8" to 12". Install inverted J-channel (without weep holes) along the eaves and gables the same way. Overlap channels ¾", following step 7 on page 119. Keep channels ¼" from corner posts.

Variation: If the exterior sheathing isn't plywood or a wood substrate that can hold nails, install 1 × 3 furring strips every 12" to 16" horizontally on the walls and around doors and windows. Nail them to studs. When installing siding, drive nails into the furring strips.

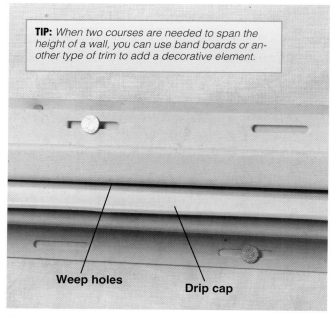

TIP: When two courses are needed to span the height of a wall, you can use band boards or another type of trim to add a decorative element.

Weep holes   **Drip cap**

3 If a single panel won't span the height of a wall, install J-channel where the first course will end, keeping a ¼" gap between the top of the siding and the channel (there should also be a ⅜" gap at the bottom of the panel). Fasten drip cap over the J-channel. Drill weep holes in J-channel and nail in place over the drip cap.

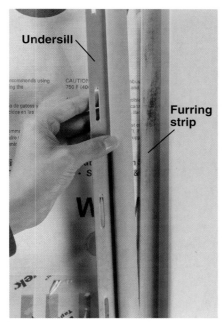

Undersill

Furring strip

4 Nail a furring strip inside the receiving channel of a corner post. Install undersill over the furring strip.

Call 1-80

Meets the ASTM E1677 Type I Air Retar...

5 Cut off the locking channel opposite the nailing flange on the first panel. Create tabs ¼" from the edge, every 6", using a snaplock punch. Snap the panel into the sill in the corner post. Keep a ¼" gap at the top and a ⅜" gap at the bottom of the panel. Use a level to make sure the panel is plumb. Nail it at the top of the uppermost slot, then every 12" in the center of the slots.

TIP: *Vertical panels expand mostly downward. When installing, keep a larger gap at the bottom than top.*

6 Place the second panel over the first, locking them together. Nail every 12". Install remaining panels the same way. Cut panels to fit around doors and windows with a ¼" gap, following steps 17 to 19 on page 122. Where needed, install furring strips over J-channels to hold panels snug in place. At the opposite corner, install a furring strip and undersill in the corner post. Rip the last panel to fit, create tabs, and slide in place.

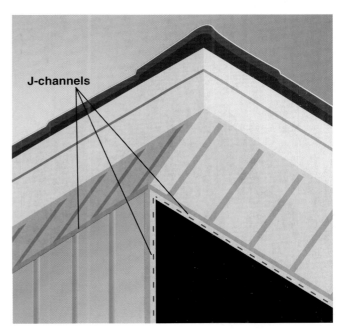

J-channels

7 For gables, mark a line straight down from the peak. Install flashing over the line. Install two J-channels, back to back, over the flashing. Cut the angle for the top of the panel, following step 21 on page 123. Cut the panel to size, keeping a ¼" gap at both ends, and install in the center channel. Install remaining panels, then do the same for the other side of the J-channel.

How to Install Vinyl Shakes

1 Follow steps 1 to 7 on pages 118 to 119 to prepare the walls, install starter strip and corner posts, trim the doors and windows, and fasten J-channel along the gable end of the house. Install J-channel under the horizontal eaves, and use channel rather than undersill under windows.

2 Cut a straight line along the non-flanged (right) edge of the first panel, using a circular saw with a carbide-tipped blade. Do not reverse the blade. If the panel has a manufacturer's mark for the cut, follow the mark. Lock the bottom of the panel over the starter strip and slide it into the corner post, keeping a ¼" gap between the panel and post.

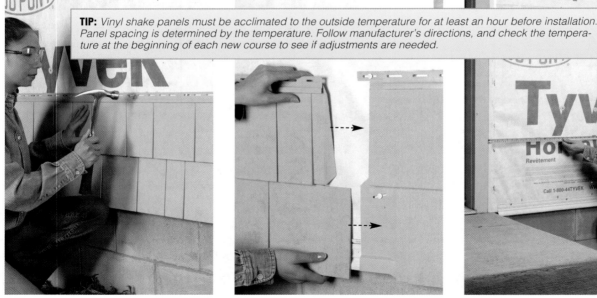

TIP: Vinyl shake panels must be acclimated to the outside temperature for at least an hour before installation. Panel spacing is determined by the temperature. Follow manufacturer's directions, and check the temperature at the beginning of each new course to see if adjustments are needed.

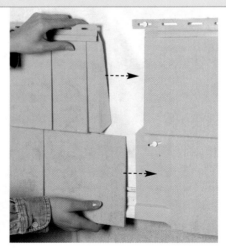

3 Follow the exact nailing sequence prescribed by the manufacturer. For this siding, it starts with the nail slot at the top right, then the top left, then the left side flange, followed by the center of the panel. Nails are then driven every 8".

4 Fit the next panel into position over the starter strip. The nailing hem and bottom half of the panel fit over the first panel; the top shakes fit under the first panel. Overlap the panels following temperature guidelines. Nail in place, using the nailing sequence.

5 Install remaining panels in the row. For the last panel, measure from the correct temperature line on the last installed panel to the corner post, and subtract ¼". Cut the panel to size along the left side and install.

Alignment line

6 Measure from the left alignment line on the first panel of the first course to the corner post, and subtract ¼". Cut a panel to this size, removing the non-flanged edge. Place the panel over the first row, snapping the lock together and pulling up so the panel is tight. Align the left side flange with the left alignment line of the underlying panel, and nail in place.

7 For the third course, measure from the right alignment line of the second panel in the second row to the corner post, and subtract ¼". Cut a panel to this size, removing the right edge. Install the panel, aligning the left side flange with the right alignment line. Install remaining rows, following step 6 for even rows and step 7 for odd rows. Cut panels to fit the opposite corner and abut doors, leaving a ¼" gap.

TIP: If the siding feels loose in the J-channel around doors, windows, or under the eaves, nail a furring strip over the channel, then install the siding over the furring strip.

8 Cut panels to fit around windows, following steps 17 to 19 on page 122. Make a nail slot every 8" along the cut edge of the panels, using a nail slot punch. Set the panel in place. Drive nails through the slots at an angle. The J-channel should hide the nail heads.

9 Measure the height for the last row of panels under the eaves, keeping a ¼" gap for movement. Rip the panels to size. Create nail slots every 8" along the cut edge. Install the panels, and nail through the slots.

Installing Lap Siding

There are several types of horizontal board siding applications, such as clapboard, tongue and groove, bevel, and shiplap, but the most popular is lap siding, which is the project we're showing here. The installation is fairly straightforward, with each course overlapping the underlying row and covering up the nailing. We're using a measuring gauge that's pre-set to give each course of siding the exact same amount of overlap.

Before installing wood siding, make sure it's acclimated to your environment so it can expand or shrink prior to being nailed in place. For our project, we're using fiber cement siding, which offers the look and texture of wood but doesn't rot or crack. The application is basically the same, although fiber cement can be more difficult to nail (you may want to pre-drill holes) and requires a carbide-tipped blade for cutting. Wear a respirator when cutting fiber cement since it contains silica, which can cause lung disease.

Store siding in a flat position, and keep it off the ground and covered until ready for use. When carrying the siding, make sure it doesn't bend and crack. Having a helper makes this job much easier. The siding panels need to be nailed to studs, so it's critical for the marks on the housewrap to be aligned with the wall studs. Cut the panels face down to avoid marring or damaging the faces.

If the siding is not yet primed, apply a coat of primer before installing. Also apply primer to cut edges during the installation process. Some wood and fiber cement siding need to be painted after they're installed. Although you'll have a paint job on your hands when the project is finished, the upside is you'll have the opportunity to change the color of your siding whenever you want by applying a new coat of paint. Other sidings are available in colors that don't require painting, and the seams are caulked with a matching colored caulk.

Everything You Need

Tools: tape measure, circular saw, caulk gun, chalk line, paint brush, combination saw blade (for wood), carbide-tipped saw blade (for fiber cement), 4-ft. level, measuring gauge, T-bevel.

Materials: ¼ × 1½" lath, siding and trim, 6d corrosion-resistant nails, 2" corrosion-resistant siding nails, flexible caulk, primer.

How to Install Lap Siding

1 Cover the exterior walls with housewrap so the stud marks fall on the studs (see pages 114 to 115). Starting at the lowest corner of the house, snap a level line at the bottom of the wall where the siding will begin. The siding should cover the sill plate, but stay above grade and concrete surfaces.

2 Install a corner trim board flush with the outside wall and flush with the chalk line at the bottom. Keep nails 1" from each end and ¾" from the edges. Drive two nails every 16". Overlap a second trim board on the adjacent side, aligning the edge with the face of the first board, and nail in place.

3 When two or more corner trim pieces are needed to complete a wall, cut a 45° bevel on the end of each board. Apply primer to the cut ends. Install the first board so the bevel faces away from the house. Place the top piece over the first board, aligning the bevels. Stagger seams between adjacent sides.

4 Place a corner trim board in an inside corner. Drive nails every 16".

(continued next page)

How to Install Lap Siding (continued)

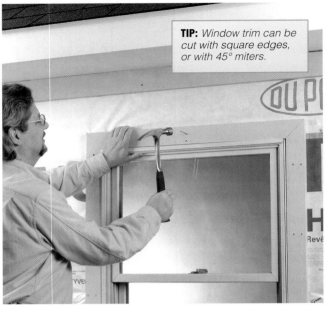

TIP: Window trim can be cut with square edges, or with 45° miters.

5 Measure and cut trim to fit around a window. Install trim along the bottom of the window first, then measure and cut trim to fit along the sides, flush with the bottom edge of the first trim piece and ⅛" above the top of the drip cap. Measure and cut trim to fit over the window, flush with the outside edges of the side trim. Drive two nails in the trim pieces every 16". Repeat for each window and door.

Option: Rather than install the trim first, wait until after the siding is in place. Then, nail the trim directly over the siding. Make sure the nails are long enough to penetrate through the siding and sheathing and into the studs by at least 1".

6 On horizontal eaves, install frieze boards directly under the soffits. Butt the frieze boards against the corner trim, and drive two nails every 16" into studs.

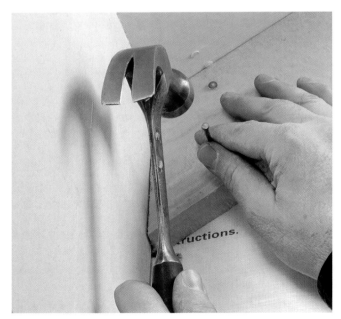

7 Use a T-bevel to determine the angle on the gable end of the house. Cut this angle on the end of a frieze board, and install under the soffits.

TIP: *Rather than buying lath, rip panels of wood or fiber cement siding to 1½"-wide strips and use them as lath.*

8 Install lath along the base of the walls. Align the bottom edge of the lath with the chalk line and nail in place, using 6d nails. Keep the lath ⅛" from the corner trim.

9 Cut the first siding panel so it ends halfway over a stud when the other end is placed ⅛" from a corner trim board. Apply primer to the cut end. Align the siding with the bottom edge of the lath. Keep a ⅛" gap between the siding and corner trim. Nail the panel at each stud location, 1" from the top edge, using siding nails.

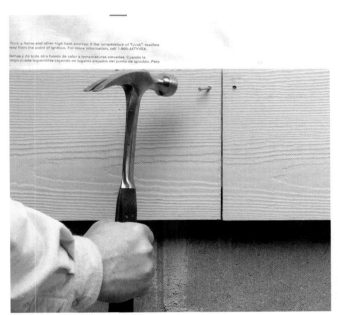

10 Measure and cut the next panel so it reaches the opposite corner or falls at the midpoint of a stud. Set the panel over the lath, keeping a ⅛" gap between the first panel and the second panel. Nail the panel ⅜" from the seam edge and at every stud.

11 Set the measuring gauge to give the panels a minimum of 1¼" overlap. Place the second row of panels over the first, using the measuring gauge to set the amount of overlap. Offset seams by at least one stud. Repeat this procedure for subsequent rows. Check every five or six rows for level. Make adjustments in small increments. Cut or notch panels as necessary to fit around protrusions in the walls.

(continued next page)

12 For windows, slide the siding panel against the bottom window trim. Mark the panel ⅛" from the outside edges of the side trim. Place a scrap piece of siding next to the window trim at the proper overlap.

Mark the depth of the cut ⅛" below the bottom trim. Transfer the measurement to the siding panel and cut it to fit. Install the cutout panel around the window. Do the same at the top of the window.

Option: Siding 12" or wider, or siding nailed 24" on center, needs to be face nailed. The siding is over-lapped a minimum of 1¼" and nailed ¾" to 1" from the bottom. Drive the nail through both planks of siding into the stud, using corrosion-resistant siding nails.

13 When installing the siding over a roof line, keep the panels 1" to 2" above the roofing. Use a T-bevel to determine the angle of the roof line, and transfer the angle to siding. Cut the panels to fit. Place the bottom edge of the siding over the roof flashing and nail the panel in place.

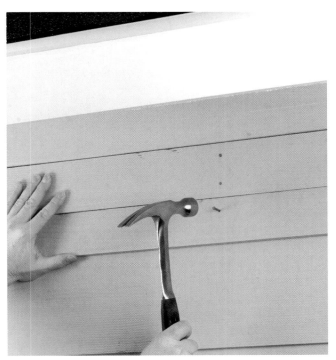

14 Rip the last row of panels to fit ⅛" below the frieze boards under the horizontal eaves. Nail the panels in place.

15 Use a T-bevel to determine the angle of the roof line on the gable ends of the house. Transfer the angle to the panels, and cut them to fit.

16 Keep the panels ⅛" from the rake boards, and nail them in place along the gable end.

17 Fill all gaps between panels and trim with flexible, paintable caulk. Paint the siding as desired (see Exterior Painting, beginning on page 198).

Wood shakes and shingles are commonly used as siding for Victorian and Cape Cod style houses, although they can be used on any type of house to create a rustic look.

Installing Wood Shakes & Shingles

The siding application for shakes and for shingles is basically the same, but there is a difference between the two materials. Shakes are hand-split, then sawn in half, giving them a rough surface and a flat, smooth back. Shingles are machine-sawn on both sides to create smooth, tapered boards that are thinner than shakes. Both shakes and shingles are typically made from cedar.

Shakes and shingles are usually installed in a pattern called single coursing, which is what's used for our project. Each piece of siding overlaps the one below. For a greater look of depth, consider the double course or staggered butt course shown on the opposite page. Likewise, there is more than one way to treat corners, with alternatives featured on the opposite page. The more overlap you have between rows, the more protection the siding provides, although it also consumes more siding materials.

Each shake or shingle is installed with two corrosion-resistant nails, most commonly 4d to 7d nails. The nail size is determined by the size and

type of shake or shingle. Check manufacturer's recommendations. The manufacturer will also specify the spacing between siding pieces. Most shakes and shingles will expand after installation, although some that are green or freshly cut may actually shrink.

The siding must be installed over sheathing that has a solid nailing surface, such as plywood. If there isn't a suitable nailing surface, install 1 × 3 or 1 × 4 furring strips across the house for nailing. Felt paper is commonly used as an underlayment, but check building codes for underlayment requirements in your area.

Everything You Need

Tools: hammer, handsaw or coping saw, tape measure, utility knife, stapler, chalk line, line level, paintbrush, T-bevel, chalk gun.

Materials: shakes or shingles, 2 × 2, 1 × 3, and 1 × 4 cedar trim boards, nails, 30# felt paper, staples, sealer, flexible caulk.

Variations for Coursing

Double-course installation offers a greater look of depth between rows. Each course of shingles is installed ½" lower than an undercourse that's placed beneath it. A lower-grade, less-expensive shingle is typically used for the undercourse.

Staggered butt-course installation features a random, three-dimensional look. The application starts with a double starter row, and shingles in overlapping courses are staggered by up to 1".

Variations for Corner Installations

Woven corners have shingles that overlap at the corners for a weave effect. This overlap alternates between walls with each successive course.

Mitered corners are made by cutting corner shingles at a 45° angle and butting them together. This method is very time consuming.

How to Install Single-course Wood Shakes & Shingles

1 Cover the exterior sheathing with felt paper. Starting at the bottom of a wall, install the paper horizontally, using staples. Wrap corners a minimum of 4". Overlap vertical seams 6" and horizontal seams 2". Cut out openings around doors and windows.

2 Starting at the lowest corner of the house, snap a level chalk line at the bottom of each wall where the siding will start. Measure the height of the wall from the chalk line to the soffits.

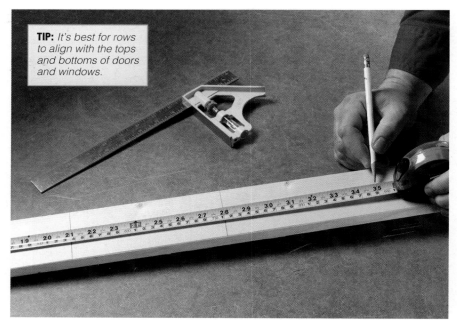

> **TIP:** *It's best for rows to align with the tops and bottoms of doors and windows.*

3 To determine the exposure of the shingles—the amount of wood revealed beneath the overlap—divide the wall height by the number of proposed rows. The goal is to find an exposure measurement that can be multiplied by a whole number to equal the wall height—a 120" wall can have 12 rows with a 10" exposure, for example. Create a story pole on a straight 1 × 3 by making a series of marks equal to the exposure.

4 Place the story pole at a corner, aligning the bottom with the chalk line. Transfer the marks onto the wall. Do this at each corner, door, and window location.

TIP: As soon as you cut a shingle or piece of trim, apply sealer to the cut edge.

5 Place a 1 × 3 board at an outside corner, aligning it with the chalk line at the bottom. Keep the outside edge flush with the adjacent wall. Nail it in place. Overlap the edge of the board with a 1 × 4, align it with the chalk line, and nail in place. If more than one trim board is needed to span the length of the wall, miter the ends at 45° and place them together. Do this for all outside corners.

6 Fasten a 2 × 2 in an inside corner, flush with the chalk line at the bottom. If more than one board is needed to span the height of the wall, miter the adjoining ends at 45° and butt them together.

7 If the chalk line is hard to see, run a string from the bottom of the corner trim pieces. Starting at a corner, install the starter row of shingles, ½" above the chalk line. Keep the manufacturer's recommended distance between shingles and between shingles and trim, usually a ⅛" to ¼" gap. Keep nails ¾" from edges and 1" above the line of exposure.

8 Place the first course of shingles over the starter row, flush with the chalk line at the bottom. Overlap the seams in the starter course by at least 1½".

(continued next page)

9 Snap a chalk line across the shingles to mark the exposure, using the reference lines from step 4. Install a course of shingles at the chalk line, offsetting the seams. Install remaining rows the same way.

Option: To ensure straight lines, tack a 1 × 4 flush with your reference lines. Nail the board through gaps between shingles. Use the board as a guide for installing the shingles.

TIP: Whenever possible, plan your layout so you can install full shingles next to doors and windows rather than cutting shingles to fit.

10 Cut shingles to fit around doors, windows, and protrusions in the walls, using a coping saw or handsaw. Make sure gaps between shingles aren't aligned with the edges of doors and windows.

11 Cut and install the tops of shingles over windows and doors. Align the tops with adjacent shingles on either side of the door or window.

12 When applying shingles on a dormer or above a roof line, keep the bottom edge of the shingles ½" above the roof shingles. Cut shingles with a handsaw or circular saw.

13 Measure and cut the last row of shingles to fit under the horizontal eaves. Leave the recommended gap between shingles and soffits. Nail the shingles in place.

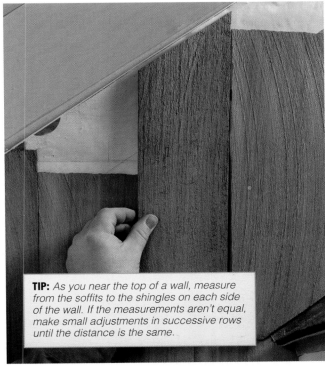

TIP: As you near the top of a wall, measure from the soffits to the shingles on each side of the wall. If the measurements aren't equal, make small adjustments in successive rows until the distance is the same.

14 Use a T-bevel to determine the roof angle on the gable end of the house. Cut shingles at this angle for each row at the gable end, using a handsaw or circular saw. Install shingles up to the peak.

15 Caulk around all doors, windows, protrusions, and corner trim. Apply your choice of stain or primer and paint (see Exterior Painting, starting on page 198).

The board and batten siding on the second level offers vertical, parallel lines that are juxtaposed against the horizontal siding on the lower level. The effect is a contrasting exterior that uses multiple colors.

Installing Board & Batten Siding

Board and batten is a vertically installed siding that offers a rustic look and makes houses appear taller. The application consists of installing wide boards vertically on the walls, then placing narrow boards, called battens, over the seams.

Although there are no set board and batten widths, a popular combination is 1 × 10" boards with 1 × 3" battens, which is what we're using for this project. Our lumber is knotty cedar, which is often used for board and batten applications.

Regardless of the type and size of lumber you choose, the battens need to overlap the boards by at least ½". To maintain a uniform look, measure the length of the wall, the width of the boards, and determine the appropriate spacing between boards so you can install a full board at the end of the wall. Ripping the last board to fit will ruin the symmetry you've established.

Before installing the siding, you'll need to install horizontal blocking lines or furring strips on the walls. This gives you a firm nailing base for the siding. Nails must be driven 1½" into solid wood.

Nailing directly to your sheathing, even if it's plywood, will not provide sufficient hold. Because the nailing strips add thickness to your walls, you'll need to extend the jambs and sills around your doors and windows.

Another way to achieve the board-on-board look is to use board and batten panels (page 145). These panels feature a reverse batten style, in which the batten is placed behind the simulated boards. The panels are typically available in 4 × 8 or 4 × 9-foot sheets to span the length of the wall. Be sure to purchase panels that are rated for exterior use.

Everything You Need

Tools: tape measure, circular saw, hammer, chalk line, line level, pry bar, tin snips, level, jig saw, T-bevel, caulk gun, 4-ft. level, paint brush.

Materials: 1 × 10 and 1 × 3 cedar lumber, 1 × 3 nailing strips, 2 × 4, 8d and 10d corrosion-resistant box nails, drip caps, 6d galvanized box nails, sealer, caulk.

How to Install Board & Batten Siding

1 Cover the walls with housewrap (pages 114 to 115). Starting at the bottom of the wall, fasten horizontal nailing strips every 16" to 24". Nail the strips to studs, using 8d nails. Install nailing strips around all doors and windows. Do this for each wall.

> **TIP:** Jamb extenders should be thick enough to be flush with the outside of the board siding when installed.

2 Carefully remove the exterior trim around windows and doors, using a pry bar. Rip jamb extenders to the same width as the jambs.

3 Cut an extender to fit over a window. Nail it in place, using nails that penetrate the jamb by at least 1". Cut and install jambs along the sides of the window, then do the same for the sill. Apply sealer to all cut edges.

4 Cut a piece of drip cap to size to fit over the window, using tin snips. Set the drip cap in place so the bottom lip is over the jamb extension. Nail the drip cap in the upper corners, using 6d galvanized nails. Repeat Steps 2 to 4 for each window and door.

(continued next page)

How to Install Board & Batten Siding (continued)

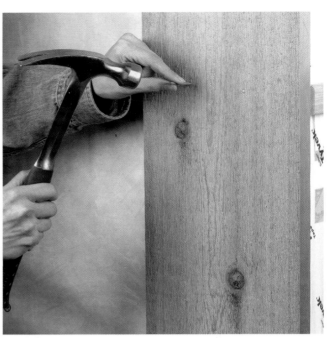

TIP: *Don't cut all boards to size at the start of a wall. The distance from the ledger to the soffits can change, which can impact the length of the boards.*

5 Starting at a corner, snap a level chalk line at the bottom of the wall where you want to start the siding. Make sure it's below the nailing strips. Install a straight 2 × 4 flush with the chalk line to use as a temporary ledger.

6 Measure from the ledger to the soffits, then subtract ⅛". Cut a siding board to this length. Set the bottom of the board on the ledger, and align the side with the edge of the wall. For boards 6" and narrower, drive one 8d nail in the center at each nailing strip. For boards wider than 6", drive two nails 3" apart.

TIP: *To maintain even spacing between boards, cut wood spacers the size of your gaps and use them when installing each board.*

7 Cut the next board to size and set in place on the ledger. Keep your predetermined gap between boards, but make sure the batten will overlap each board by at least ½". Nail in place at each nailing strip. Install remaining boards the same way. Check every few boards with a level to make sure they're plumb. If they're not, adjust slightly until plumb.

8 At window locations, set a board next to the window, keeping the bottom on the ledger. Mark the board ⅛" above and below the outside of the top and bottom jambs.

9 Position a scrap board under the window, keeping the proper gap from the last installed board. Mark the scrap board ⅛" past the outside edge of the side jamb. Use this measurement to mark the cutout on the board you marked in step 8. Cut out the window opening, using a jig saw.

10 Set the board in place, keeping a ⅛" gap around the window jamb. When installing, drive only one nail per nailing strip in the area next to the window. Repeat steps 8 to 10 for each window and door.

11 If more than one board is needed to span the height of a wall, cut a 45° bevel in the ends of the adjoining boards and butt them together. Make sure the seam falls over a nailing strip. Offset seams by at least one nailing strip. Note: Whenever possible, use full-length boards rather than butting two boards together.

12 When starting a new wall, place the first board over the edge of the last installed board on the adjacent wall. Nail the board in place.

(continued next page)

How to Install Board & Batten Siding (continued)

13 At the gable end of the house, use a T-bevel to determine the pitch of the roof. Transfer the angle to the boards, cut to size, and install. The length of each board needs to be measured individually since the distance changes along the gable end.

14 Fill gaps between the boards and soffits, and between the boards and jambs with flexible, paintable caulk.

15 Measure and cut battens to size. Center a batten over each gap between boards. Drive one 10d nail in the battens at each nailing strip. Once the battens are installed, remove the ledger board. Paint the siding (see Exterior Painting, starting on page 198).

Variation: To create a deep channel look, install the battens first, then place the boards over the battens.

How to Install Board & Batten Paneling

TIP: *When nailing, drive nails through studs every 6" along the edges and every 10" in the field.*

1 Cover the walls with house-wrap (pages 114 to 116). Snap a level line at the base of the wall where the siding will start. Install a straight ledger board flush with the line, following step 5 on page 142.

2 Starting at a corner, measure from the ledger to the soffits, subtract ⅛", and cut the panel to size. Place the panel on the ledger, flush with the corner, and install, using corrosion-resistant nails that penetrate studs by 1½".

3 If the panels have built-in ship-laps, overlap the panels as specified by the manufacturer. If the panels don't have laps, leave ⅛" gaps between panels.

4 Place a panel next to a window and make a mark ⅛" above and below the outside of the jambs. Set a scrap piece in place under the window and make a mark ⅛" past the side jambs. Transfer the measurements to the panel, then cut out the window opening, using a jig saw. Do the same for each door, window, and protrusion.

5 Follow steps 13 and 14 on page 144 to cut panels to fit the gable end of the house, and to caulk between panels and soffits. To create a more finished look, install 1 × 3 or 1 × 4 trim around doors, windows, and corners, and under soffits. Paint the siding (see Exterior Painting, starting on page 198).

This house isn't really a log cabin, but you'd never know it from the outside. The log cabin siding provides the charm and realism of an actual log home.

(Photo courtesy of Midwest Lumber)

Installing Log Cabin Siding

Log cabin siding is an inexpensive way to achieve the rustic look of log homes. Since the siding is not composed of full logs, it uses less wood, making it less expensive than traditional log cabins. But from the outside, it's almost impossible to tell that the house is not an actual log cabin. The log-tail corners complete the authentic appearance. Where the log tails would restrict a pathway or entrance, or create a design problem, vertical log corners can be used.

Log cabin siding is generally available in cedar or pine. For our project, we're using 2 x 8 pine siding, which is considerably less expensive than cedar. The siding is face nailed, but the nails are hardly visible. To speed up installation, rent an air compressor and nail gun. If you choose to hand nail, be sure to use a hammer with a smooth face. A corrugated face could mar the siding.

You can cut the siding with a circular saw, but a compound saw or miter saw works better. It's critical for the cuts to be square since the siding pieces butt against each other. The siding must be nailed to studs, so be sure the stud marks on the housewrap are properly aligned with the studs in the walls.

Everything You Need

Tools: hammer, level, chalk line, chisel, tape measure, drill, 4-ft. level, caulk gun, jig saw, miter saw or sliding compound saw, T-bevel, paintbrush.

Materials: log cabin siding, cedar or pine 2 x 2s, 2 x 4s, 2 x 6s, housewrap, cap nails, left- and right- side corners, 12d or 16d hot-dipped galvanized siding nails, polyurethane caulk, sealer.

How to Install Log Cabin Siding

1 Cover the walls with housewrap (pages 114 to 115) and snap a level line around the base of the walls for the first row of siding, following step 1 on page 129. Place a 2 × 2 in each inside corner, flush with the chalk line at the bottom, and nail in place. If more than one 2 × 2 is needed to span the wall, cut a 45° bevel at the joining ends.

2 Use 2 × 2s or 2 × 4s to trim doors and windows. Measure the top, bottom, and sides of doors and windows, add ¼" to each piece, and cut to size. Install the trim, keeping a ⅛" gap between the window and door frames and the trim.

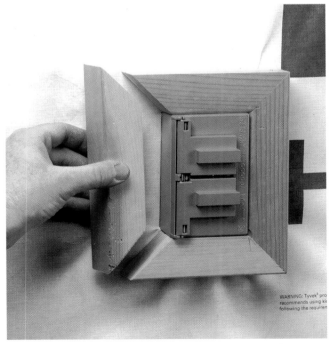

3 Apply 2 × 2 trim around electrical outlets, the electric meter, and vents.

Option: If using vertical corners, place the corner on the wall, flush with the chalk line at the bottom, and nail in place. Install vertical corners before applying any siding. Keep siding ⅛" from these corners.

(continued next page)

How to Install Log Cabin Siding (continued)

TIP: Apply sealer to the cut ends of siding, trim, and corners before installing.

4 Hold a piece of siding in place with the bottom (groove) edge aligned with the chalk line and the end flush with an outside corner. Mark the opposite end at the midpoint of the last stud it crosses. Cut the siding at the mark. Apply sealer to the cut end.

5 Set the siding back in place along the chalk line, flush with the corner. Fasten it to the wall with two siding nails at each stud location. Drive the first nail 1½" from the bottom edge, and the second nail 3" to 4" above that. Cut the next piece to reach the opposite corner, butt it against the first piece, and install.

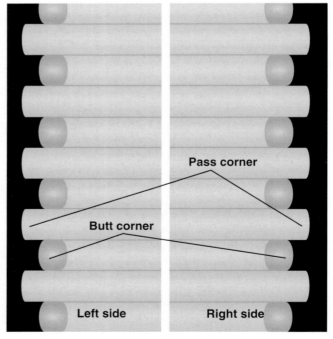

Pass corner

Butt corner

Left side

Right side

6 On the adjacent wall, start with a corner piece. Hold it in place so the log tail overlaps the adjacent siding. Mark the opposite end at the last stud. Cut it to length, set along the chalk line so the corner overlaps the adjacent wall, and nail in place. Install the remaining first course the same way.

7 Alternate between the butt and the pass at the corners for each row of siding. The corners at both ends of a wall must be the same, either both butts or both passes, for each course. You cannot have a butt at one end of the wall and a pass at the opposite corner.

TIP: *There are left-side and right-side corner pieces. Be sure to use the correct piece for each corner. Start the siding on a wall that has a "butt" corner, then overlap it with a "pass" on the adjacent side. For a butt corner, the end of the siding is flush with the corner. A pass corner extends past the corner to overlap siding on the adjacent wall.*

8 Place the second row of siding over the first, setting the groove over the lip of the siding below. Offset joints between rows by at least two studs. Keep a ⅛" gap between the siding and inside corners. Install remaining courses the same way.

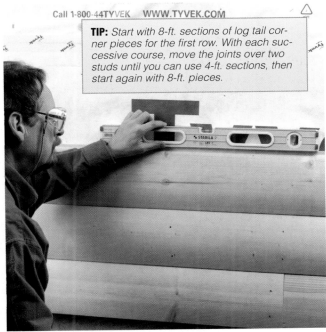

TIP: *Start with 8-ft. sections of log tail corner pieces for the first row. With each successive course, move the joints over two studs until you can use 4-ft. sections, then start again with 8-ft. pieces.*

9 For hose spigots and other small wall protrusions that you don't frame around, drill a hole in the siding at the proper location, then place the siding over the object. To keep the hole as small as possible, you may need to remove the protrusion, then reinsert it after the siding is in place.

10 Check every few rows of siding with a level. If necessary, leave a small gap between the grooves and lips in the siding until the rows are level. Make the changes subtly over several courses.

(continued next page)

11 Install siding up to the bottom of windows. Hold a piece of siding in place below the window framing. Make a mark on the siding, ⅛" past the outside edge of the side window trim. Place a scrap of siding next to the window, over the last installed row. Mark the siding piece, ⅛" below the edge of the window.

12 Transfer the measurements from the last step to a piece of siding. Cut out the opening, using a jig saw.

TIP: For optimum appearance, keep joints in the siding from falling directly above or below windows and doors.

13 Install the siding, keeping a ⅛" gap around the window frame. As you continue installing rows of siding, maintain a ⅛" gap between the siding and trim.

14 Follow steps 11 to 12 to mark and cut siding to fit over the top of doors and windows. Center the siding opening over the door and window, and nail in place.

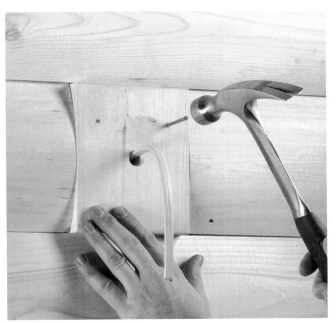

15 At light fixture locations, drill a hole in the siding for electrical wires. To make a flat surface to hold the fixture, start at the wire hole and work out 2¾" on each side, making a series of 1"-deep cuts in the siding. Chisel out the wood until the surface is flat, and apply sealer. Install the siding, feeding the wires through the hole. Cut a 2 × 6 the height of the siding, drill a hole for the wiring, and install in the notch. Mount the fixture on the 2 × 6.

16 For the top row, measure the distance from the bottom of the lip of the last installed row of siding to the eaves. Subtract ⅛" and rip siding to this measurement. Nail the siding in place under the eaves.

17 On the gable ends of the house, use a T-bevel to determine the roof angle. Cut the ends of the siding at this angle, then install along the gable.

18 Caulk between the siding and inside corners. Also caulk between siding and vertical corners, siding and window and door framing, and around wall protrusions. Do not apply caulk to the joints between siding. Stain the siding, following the instructions on pages 218 to 219.

Working With Mortar

Handling mortar is a skill you'll need when working with stucco, brick, veneer stone, or concrete block. Although "throwing mortar" is an acquired skill that takes years to perfect, you can use the basic techniques successfully with just a little practice.

The first critical element to handling mortar effectively is the mixture. If it's too thick, it will fall off the trowel in a heap, not in the smooth line that is your goal. Add too much water, and the mortar becomes messy and weak. Follow the manufacturer's directions, but keep in mind that the amount of water specified is an approximation. If you've never mixed mortar before, experiment with small amounts until you find a mixture that clings to the trowel just long enough for you to deliver a controlled, even line that holds its shape after settling. Note how much water you use in each batch, and record the best mixture.

Mix mortar for a large project in batches. On a hot, dry day, a large batch will harden before you know it. If mortar begins to thicken, add water (called retempering). Use retempered mortar within two hours.

Throwing mortar is a quick, smooth technique that requires practice. Load the trowel with mortar, then position the trowel a few inches above the starting point. In one motion, begin turning your wrist over and quickly move the trowel across the surface to spread mortar consistently. Proper mortar-throwing results in a rounded line about 2½" wide and about 2 ft. long.

Everything You Need

Tools: mason's trowel, masonry hoe, shovel, mortar box.

Materials: mortar mix, plywood, blocks.

Selecting the Right Mortar

Masonry mortar is a mixture of portland cement, sand, and water. Ingredients such as lime and gypsum are added to improve workability or control "setup" time. Every mortar mixture balances strength, workability, and other qualities. The strongest mortar is not always the best one for the job. A mortar that's too strong won't absorb stresses, such as those that occur as temperatures rise and fall. The result can be damage to masonry structures.

Always follow the guidelines for your project and the materials you've selected, and read the manufacturer's specifications on the mortar mix package. The information below indicates the typical uses for the most commonly sold mortar mixes. Type N mortar mix is called for most often because it offers a good blend of strength and workability.

Types of Mortar & Their Uses

Gone are the days when do-it-yourselfers had to mix mortar from scratch. These days, when you think of mortar, think of mortar mix, the standard term for the dry, prepackaged mixes available at home centers. For most of today's projects, simply select the proper mortar mixture, mix in water, and start to trowel. For some repair projects, adding a fortifier may be recommended. You can also tint your mortar to match your other materials.

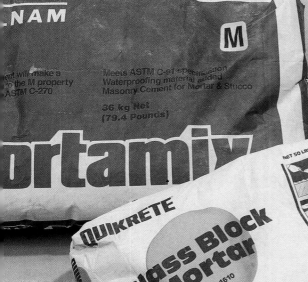

Type N
Medium-strength mortar for above grade outdoor use in non-load-bearing (freestanding) walls, barbecues, chimneys, soft stone masonry, and tuck-pointing.

Type S
High-strength mortar for exterior use at or below grade. Generally used in foundations, brick and block retaining walls, driveways, walks, and patios.

Type M
Very high-strength specialty mortar for load-bearing exterior stone walls, including stone retaining walls and veneer applications.

Refractory Mortar
A calcium aluminate mortar that does not break down with exposure to high temperatures. It's used for mortaring around firebrick in fireplaces and barbecues. Chemical-set mortar is best because it will cure even in wet conditions.

Glass Block Mortar
A specialty white Type S mortar for glass block projects. Standard gray Type S mortar is also acceptable for glass block projects.

How to Mix & Throw Mortar

TIP: *Don't mix too much mortar at one time. Mortar is much easier to work with when it's fresh.*

1 Empty mortar mix into a mortar box and form a depression in the center. Add about ¾ of the recommended amount of water into the depression, then mix it in with a masonry hoe. Don't overwork the mortar. Continue adding small amounts of water and mixing until the mortar reaches the proper consistency.

2 Set a piece of plywood on blocks at a convenient height, and place a shovelful of mortar onto the surface. Slice off a strip of mortar from the pile, using the edge of your mason's trowel. Slip the trowel point-first under the section of mortar and lift it up.

3 Snap the trowel gently downward to dislodge excess mortar clinging to the edges. Position the trowel at the starting point, and "throw" a line of mortar onto the building surface. A good amount is enough to set three bricks. Don't get ahead of yourself. If you throw too much mortar, it will set before you're ready.

4 "Furrow" the mortar line by dragging the point of the trowel through the center of the mortar line in a slight back-and-forth motion. Furrowing helps distribute the mortar evenly.

Tips for Using Mortar with Stone

TIP: *If mortar dries too fast, strength is compromised. Cover mortared surfaces as soon as you finish a section, and keep covered for 48 hours. In hot, dry weather, lift the plastic occasionally and mist the surfaces with a fine spray.*

Mortar-set stone projects require more mortar than similar projects using brick or block because stones have highly irregular surfaces. Butter the mating surfaces of stones generously to fill in the peaks and valleys in each stone's surface.

Practice buttering stones so that each buttered surface fills the gap between one stone and the next. If the mating (adjoining) surfaces are highly contoured, butter both surfaces. You can also use the trowel to create a mound (above) or a depression to conform to the shape of the adjacent stone.

Tips for Special Mortar Treatments

Adding tint to mortar works best if you add the same amount to each batch throughout the project. Once you settle on a recipe, record it so you can mix the same proportions each time.

Use a stiff (dry) mix of mortar for tuck-pointing—it's less likely to shrink and crack. Start by mixing Type N mortar mix with half the recommended water. Let the mixture stand for one hour, then add the remaining water and finish mixing.

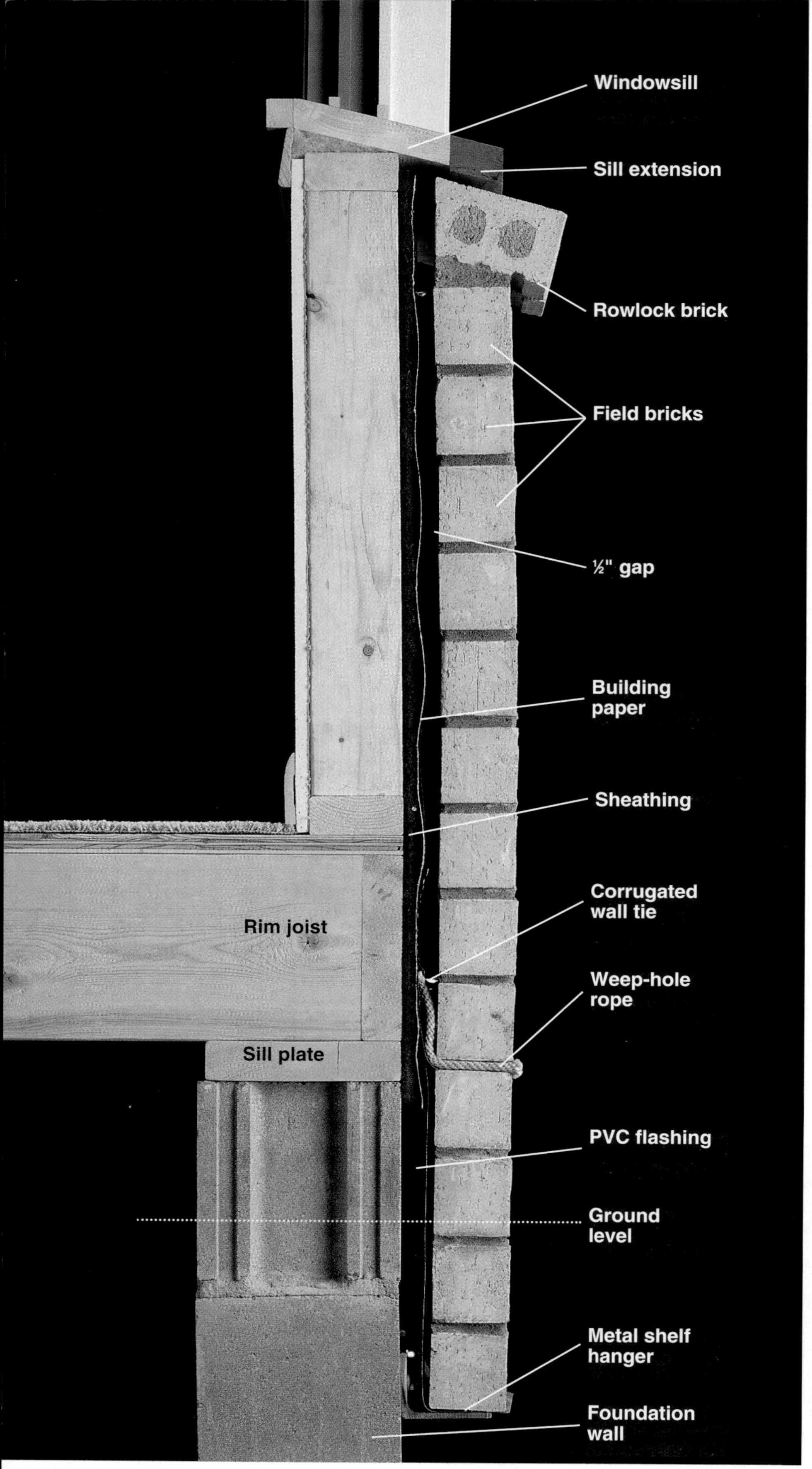

Finishing Walls with Brick

Brick veneer is essentially a brick wall built around the exterior walls of a house. It's attached to the house with metal wall ties and supported by a metal shelf hanger on the foundation. It's best to use queen-sized bricks for veneer projects because they're thinner than standard construction bricks. This means less weight for the house walls to support. Even so, brick veneer is quite heavy. Ask your local building inspector about building code rules that apply to your project. In the project shown here, brick veneer is installed over the foundation walls and side walls, up to the bottom of the windowsills on the first floor of the house. The siding materials in these areas are removed before installing the brick.

Construct a story pole before you start laying the brick so you can check your work as you go along to be sure your mortar joints are of a consistent thickness. A standard ⅜" gap is used in the project shown here.

Everything You Need

Tools: hammer, circular saw, combination square, level, drill with masonry bit, socket wrench set, staple gun, mason's trowel, masonry hoe, mortar box, mason's chisel, maul.

Materials: pressure-treated 2 × 4s, ⅜ × 4" lag screws and washers, 2 × 2, lead sleeve anchors, angle iron for metal shelf supports, 30 mil PVC roll flashing, corrugated metal wall ties, brickmold for sill extensions, sill-nosing trim, Type N mortar, bricks, ⅜-dia. cotton rope.

Windowsill
Sill extension
Rowlock brick
Field bricks
½" gap
Building paper
Sheathing
Corrugated wall tie
Weep-hole rope
PVC flashing
Ground level
Metal shelf hanger
Foundation wall
Rim joist
Sill plate

Anatomy of a brick veneer facade: Queen-sized bricks are stacked onto a metal or concrete shelf and connected to the foundation and walls with metal ties. Rowlock bricks are cut to follow the slope of the windowsills, then laid on edge over the top course of bricks.

How to Install Brick Veneer

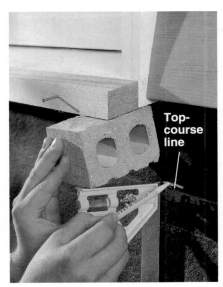

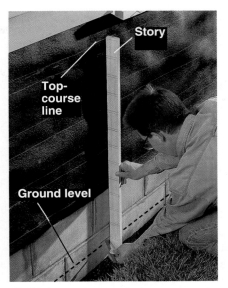

1 Remove all siding materials in the area you plan to finish with brick veneer. Before laying out the project, cut the sill extension from a pressure-treated 2 × 4. Tack the extension to the sill temporarily.

2 Precut the bricks to follow the slope of the sill and overhang the field brick by 2". Position this rowlock brick directly under the sill extension. Use a combination square or level to transfer the lowest point on the brick onto the sheathing (marking the height for the top course of brick in the field). Use a level to extend the line. Remove the sill extensions.

3 Make a story pole long enough to span the project area. Mark the pole with ⅜" joints between bricks. Dig a 12"-wide, 12"-deep trench next to the wall. Position the pole so the top-course line on the sheathing aligns with a top mark for a brick on the pole. Mark a line for the first course on the wall, below ground level.

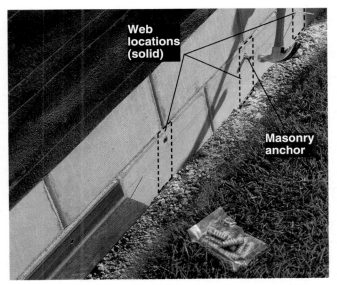

4 Extend the mark for the first-course height across the foundation wall, using a level as a guide. Measure the thickness of the metal shelf (usually ¼"), and drill pilot holes for 10d nails into the foundation at 16" intervals along the first-course line, far enough below the line to allow for the thickness of the shelf. Slip nails into the pilot holes to create temporary support for the shelf.

5 Set the metal shelf onto the temporary supports. Mark the location of the center web of each block onto the vertical face of the shelf. Remove the shelf and drill ⅜"-diameter holes for lag screws at the web marks. Set the shelf back onto the temporary supports and outline the predrilled holes on the blocks. Remove the shelf and drill holes for the masonry anchors into the foundation, using a masonry bit. Drive masonry anchors into the holes.

(continued next page)

6 Reposition the shelf on the supports so the predrilled holes align with the masonry anchors. Attach the shelf to the foundation wall with ⅜ × 4" lag screws and washers. Allow ¹⁄₁₆" for an expansion joint between shelf sections. Remove the temporary support nails.

7 After all sections of the metal shelf are attached, staple 30 mil PVC flashing above the foundation wall so it overlaps the metal shelf.

8 Test-fit the first course on the shelf. Work in from the ends, using spacers to set the gaps between bricks. You may need to cut the final brick for the course. Or, choose a pattern such as running bond that uses cut bricks.

9 Build up the corners two courses above ground level, then attach line blocks and mason's string to the end bricks. Fill in the field bricks so they align with the strings. Every 30 minutes, smooth mortar joints that are firm.

10 Attach another course of PVC flashing to the wall so it covers the top course of bricks, then staple building paper to the wall so it overlaps the top edge of the PVC flashing by at least 12". Mark wall-stud locations on the building paper.

11 Use the story pole to mark layout lines for the tops of every fifth course of bricks. Attach corrugated metal wall ties to the sheathing where the brick lines meet the marked wall-stud locations.

12 Fill in the next course of bricks, applying mortar directly onto the PVC flashing. At every third mortar joint in this course, tack a 10" piece of ⅜"-dia. cotton rope to the sheathing so it extends all the way through the bottom of the joint, creating a weep hole for drainage. Embed the metal wall ties in the mortar beds applied to this course.

13 Add courses of bricks, building up corners first, then filling in the field. Imbed the wall ties into the mortar beds as you reach them. Use corner blocks and a mason's string to verify the alignment, and check frequently with a 4-ft. level to make sure the veneer is plumb.

14 Apply a ½"-thick mortar bed to the top course, and begin laying the rowlock bricks with the cut ends against the wall. Apply a layer of mortar to the bottom of each rowlock brick, then press the brick up against the sheathing, with the top edge following the slope of the windowsills.

Sill-nosing trim

15 Finish-nail the sill extensions (step 1, page 161) to the windowsills. Nail sill-nosing trim to the siding to cover any gaps above the rowlock course. Fill cores of exposed rowlock blocks with mortar, and caulk any gaps around the veneer with silicone caulk.

Find the square footage of veneer stone required for your project by multiplying the length by the height of the area. Subtract the square footage of window and door openings and corner pieces. One linear foot of corner pieces covers approximately ¾ of a square foot of flat area, so you can reduce the square footage of flat stone required by ¾ sq. ft. for each linear foot of inside or outside corner. It's best to increase your estimate by 5 to 10 percent to allow for trimming.

Finishing Walls with Veneer Stone

If you want the look of stone on your house without the rigors of cutting and moving heavy materials, veneer stone is ideal. Two types of veneer are available. One is natural stone that has been cut into thin pieces designed for finishing walls, hearths, and other surfaces. The other is made from concrete that's molded and tinted to look like natural stone, but it's even lighter and easier to apply to these surfaces.

Whether you use natural or manufactured veneer, wet each stone, then apply mortar to the back before pressing it onto the mortared wall. Wetting and mortaring a stone (called parging) results in maximum adhesion between the stone and the wall. The challenge is to arrange the stones so that large and small stones and various hues and shapes alternate across the span of the wall.

This project is designed for installing veneer stone over plywood sheathing, which has the strength to support layers of building paper, lath, and veneer. If your walls are covered with fiberboard or any other type of sheathing, ask the veneer manufacturer for recommendations.

Note: Installing from the top down makes cleanup easier since it reduces the amount of splatter on preceding courses. However, manufacturers advise bottom-up installation for some veneers. Read the manufacturer's guidelines carefully before you begin.

Everything You Need

Tools: hammer or staple gun, drill, wheelbarrow, hoe, square-end trowel, circular saw, wide-mouth nippers or mason's hammer, dust mask, level, jointing tool, mortar bag, spray bottle, whisk broom.

Materials: Type M mortar mix, mortar tint (optional), 15# building paper, expanded galvanized metal lath (diamond mesh, minimum 2.5#), 1½" (minimum) galvanized roofing nails or heavy-duty staples, 2 × 4 lumber.

How to Finish Walls with Stone Veneer

1 Cover the wall with building paper, overlapping seams by 4". Nail or staple lath every 6" into the wall studs and midway between studs. Nails or staples should penetrate 1" into the studs. Paper and lath must extend at least 16" around corners where veneer is installed.

2 Stake a level 2 × 4 against the foundation as a temporary ledger to keep the bottom edge of the veneer 4" above grade. The gap between the bottom course and the ground will reduce staining of the veneer by plants and soil.

3 Spread out the materials on the ground so you can select pieces of varying size, shape, and color, and create contrast in the overall appearance. Alternate the use of large and small, heavily textured and smooth, and thick and thin pieces.

4 Mix a batch of Type M mortar that's firm, but still moist. Mortar that's too dry or too wet is hard to work with and may fail to bond properly.

(continued on next page)

TIP: *Mix in small amounts of water to retemper mortar that has begun to thicken.*

5 Use a square-end trowel to press a ½" to ¾" layer of mortar into the lath. To ensure that mortar doesn't set up too quickly, start with a 5 sq. ft. area. Once you determine your pace, you can mortar larger areas.

6 Install corner pieces first, alternating long and short legs. Wet and parge each piece, then press it firmly against the freshly mortared wall so some mortar squeezes out. Joints between stones should be no wider than ½" and should remain as consistent as possible across the wall.

7 Once the corner pieces are in place, install flat pieces, working from the corner toward the center of the wall.

8 If mortar becomes smeared on a stone, remove it with a whisk broom or soft-bristle brush after the mortar has begun to dry. Never use a wire brush or a wet brush of any kind.

9 Use wide-mouth nippers or a mason's hammer to trim and shape pieces to fit. Do your best to limit trimming so each piece retains its natural look.

10 You can hide cut edges that are well above or below eye level simply by rotating a stone. If an edge remains visible, use mortar to cover. Let the mortar cure for 24 hours, then remove the 2 × 4 and stakes, taking care not to dislodge any stones.

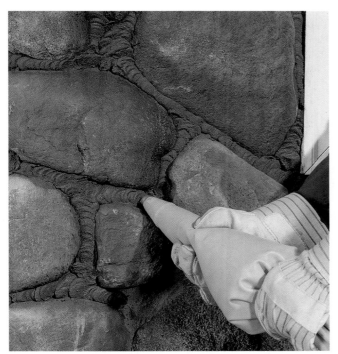

11 Once the wall is covered in veneer, fill in the joints, using a mortar bag and tuck-pointing mortar. Take extra care to avoid smearing the mortar. You can tint the tuck-pointing mortar to complement the veneer.

12 Smooth the joints with a jointing tool once the mortar is firm. Once the mortar is dry to the touch, use a dry whisk broom to remove loose mortar—water or chemicals can leave permanent stains.

Ingredients of scratch (base) coat, and brown coat stucco

3 parts sand
2 parts portland cement
1 part masonry cement
Water

Ingredients of finish coat stucco

1 part lime
3 parts sand
6 parts white cement
Tint (as desired)
Water

Portland cement

Water

Sand

Lime

Preformulated stucco mix

Combine dry stucco mix with water, following the manufacturer's directions for each coat. For the finish coat, mix a test batch first. Add measured amounts of stucco and tint until you find the proper combination.

Record the recipe, so you can repeat it for subsequent batches. A finish coat requires slightly more water than other coats.

Working with Stucco

Working with stucco is a craft that's been practiced for hundreds of years. Today's stucco is a combination of portland cement, masonry cement, sand, and (in the finish coat) lime, all mixed with water. The dry ingredients are widely available in premixed bags. The mixture is applied to walls and worked with either a trowel or a brush to achieve the desired effect.

Stuccoing an entire house from scratch is a demanding proposition, but repairing or remodeling small sections is not difficult. Walls that are kept in good condition and "redashed" occasionally with a restorative coat can last for decades.

Stucco can be applied to masonry surfaces, such as concrete block, or over wood or other materials that have been covered with building paper and metal lath. When applying stucco over

brick or block, two coats—a ⅜"-thick base coat and a ¼"-thick finish coat—are applied. When applying it over building paper and metal lath, three coats are applied—a scratch coat (⅜"-½" thick), a brown coat (⅜" thick), and a finish coat (⅛" thick).

Follow manufacturer's instructions regarding drying times between coats.

Everything You Need

Tools: cement mixer, mortar hawk, square-end trowel, hammer, stapler, utility knife, aviation snips, shovel, bucket, whisk broom, metal rake.

Materials: 15# building paper, self-furring expanded metal lath, edging, drip screed, 1½" galvanized roofing nails or heavy-duty staples, stucco mix.

164

Tips for Preparing Surfaces for Stucco

Attach building paper to wood frame construction, using heavy-duty staples or roofing nails. Overlap seams by 4". In some regions, more than one layer of building paper may be required. Ask your local building inspector about code specifications.

Install self-furring expanded metal lath over the building paper with 1½" roofing nails driven into studs every 6". Sheets of lath should overlap 1" horizontally and 2" vertically. Make sure the lath is installed with the rougher side facing out.

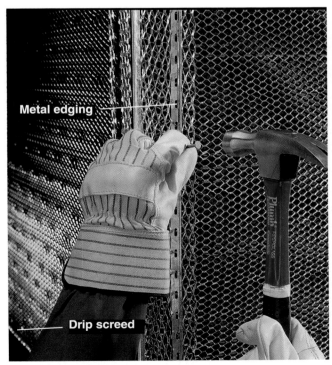

Metal edging

Drip screed

Install metal edging along edges of walls, and drip screed (also called weep screed) at the base to achieve clean corners and edges. Make sure edging is level and plumb, then attach it with roofing nails.

Use aviation snips to trim the excess lath, edging, and drip screed. Wear safety goggles and heavy gloves as protection from sharp edges.

Tips for Preparing Surfaces for Stucco

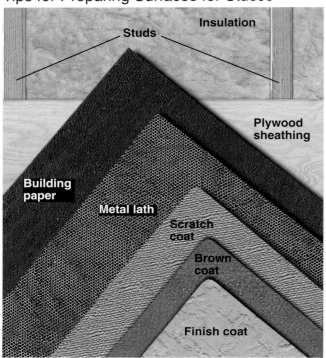

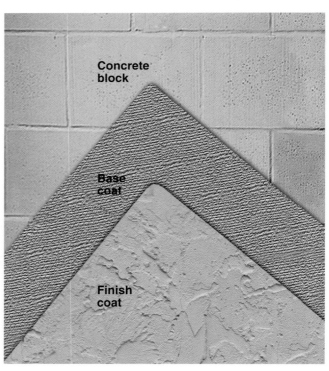

Surface preparation and the number of coats of stucco vary, depending on wall construction. A wood frame construction or insulation board surface must be covered with building paper and lath, then plastered with three coats of stucco. Stucco can be plastered directly onto concrete block, using two coats.

Tips for Applying Stucco

Use a power cement mixer for large projects. Add water to the mix until it forms a workable paste, following manufacturer's instructions.

Begin at the top or the bottom of the wall. Hold a mortar hawk close to the wall, and press stucco into the lath with a square-end trowel. Press firmly to fill voids, and cover the mesh as smoothly as possible.

Tips for Finishing Stucco

Develop a formula that yields a consistent color and texture. Test finish batches first by applying them to a scrap of wood. Let the samples dry for at least an hour for an indication of their color after the stucco has cured. Record the proper proportions.

Mix the finish batch so it contains slightly more water than the scratch and brown coats. The mix should still stay on the mortar hawk without running.

Achieve a wet-dash finish by flinging, or dashing, stucco onto the surface. Let the stucco cure undisturbed.

For a dash-trowel texture, dash the surface with stucco, using a whisk broom (left), then flatten the stucco by troweling over it.

By adding tint to the mixture, you can produce just about any color stucco you desire, from a subtle off-white to a stately blue.

Everything You Need

Tools: cement mixer, wheelbarrow, mortar hawk, mason's trowel, square-end trowel, darby or long wood float, hammer, staple gun, level, utility knife, aviation snips, spade, bucket, fine-tined metal rake.

Materials: building paper, expanded galvanized metal lath (diamond mesh, minimum 2.5 lb.), 1½" galvanized nails, 1½" wire nails, staples, stucco mix, 1½" wire nails, 1 × 2 board.

Finishing Walls with Stucco

Refinishing an entire house with stucco is a demanding job not well suited to even the most committed homeowner. It's a job best left to a stucco mason, who can complete most stucco projects in less than a week. But finishing the walls of a small addition, garage, or shed can be quite satisfying. You can use stucco to match existing walls or to create a texture that complements stone, cedar shakes, or other types of siding.

Good wall preparation is the first step for an attractive, durable finish. If the walls are wood, attach building paper and metal lath to create a tight seal and a gripping surface for the stucco. Concrete block walls are already fairly watertight and are rough enough that stucco can be applied directly to the block. During new block construction, make the mortar joints flush with the blocks in preparation for a stucco finish.

Once you've prepared the wall surface, plan to spend several days applying the three stucco coats—scratch coat, brown coat, and finish coat—that guarantee a tight seal and a professional appearance.

If the original walls of your house are finished with stucco, you'll probably need to tint your finish coat to match. Even if the stucco originally applied to your house was white, that finish has probably darkened considerably. Tinting is the best way to match the new with the old. Follow the manufacturer's instructions for the tint you purchase, and plan to experiment until you find a good match. Let each test batch dry thoroughly before you settle on the proportions. Keep notes as you test so you can reproduce the results for each subsequent batch of stucco.

How to Finish Walls with Stucco

1 Staple building paper to the entire wall, and trim excess with a utility knife. Trim the lath and edging to size, using aviation snips, and nail them to the wall. Rub your hand down the lath—it will feel rough when positioned upright. Check the edging for level.

2 Mix the scratch coat by adding water and kneading it with a trowel to form a workable paste. Beginning at either the top or the bottom of the wall, hold the mortar hawk close to the wall and press mud into the mesh with a square-end trowel. Press firmly to fill any voids. Cover the mesh completely.

TIP: *You can make a scratching tool by pounding a row of 1½" wire nails through a 1 × 2.*

3 Wait for the scratch coat to harden enough so an impression remains when you press on it. Rough up the surface by making shallow horizontal scratches the length of the wall.

4 Mist the surface occasionally for 48 hours. Mix and apply the brown coat approximately ⅜" thick, then level the entire surface with a wood darby to provide a roughened gripping surface for the finish coat.

5 Mix the finish coat, adding tint as required, and slightly more water than in previous coats. The mix should still sit on the mortar hawk without running. Apply the finish coat so the edging is fully embedded (about ⅛" thick).

6 Finish the surface by throwing stucco at the wall with a whisk broom, then flattening the stucco with a trowel. Wait 24 hours for the finish coat to set up, then mist 2 to 3 times a day for two days, and once a day for another three days.

Mix small batches of dry surface bonding cement, water, and concrete acrylic fortifier, according to the manufacturer's instructions, until you get a feel for how much coating you can apply before it hardens.

An accelerant in the cement causes the mix to harden quickly—within 30 to 90 minutes, depending on weather conditions. The cement can be tinted before application.

Finishing Walls with Cement

Surface bonding cement is a stucco-like compound that you can use to dress up your concrete and cinder block walls. It also adds strength, durability, and water resistance to the walls.

What distinguishes surface bonding cement from stucco is the addition of fiberglass to the blend of portland cement and sand. The dry mixture is combined with water and acrylic fortifier to form a cement plaster that can bond with concrete, brick, or block for an attractive, water-resistant coating.

Before applying the bonding cement, make sure you have a very clean surface, with no crumbling masonry, so the coating can form a durable bond. Because surface bonding cement dries quickly, it's important to mist the brick or block with water before applying the cement so the

cement dries slowly. As with most masonry projects, the need to dampen the wall increases in very dry weather.

The bonding cement can be used on both mortared and mortarless walls, and on both load bearing and non-load bearing walls. However, it is not recommended for walls higher than 15 courses of block.

Everything You Need

Tools: garden hose with spray attachment, bucket, wheelbarrow, mortar hawk, square-end trowel, groover, caulk gun.

Materials: surface bonding cement, concrete acrylic fortifier, tint (optional), silicone caulk.

How to Finish Walls with Surface-bonding Cement

1 Starting near the top of the wall, mist a 2 × 5-ft. section on one side of the wall with water to prevent the blocks from absorbing moisture from the cement once the coating is applied.

2 Mix the cement in small batches, according to the manufacturer's instructions, and apply a ¹⁄₁₆"- to ⅛"-thick layer to the damp blocks, using a square-end trowel. Spread the cement evenly by angling the trowel slightly and making broad upward strokes.

3 Use a wet trowel to smooth the surface and create the texture of your choice. Rinse the trowel frequently to keep it clean and wet.

4 To prevent random cracking, use a groover to cut control joints from the top to the bottom of the wall, every 4 ft. for a 2-ft.-high wall, and every 8 ft. for a 4-ft.-high wall. Seal hardened joints with silicone caulk.

Installing Shutters

Up until the last 60 years or so, window shutters were primarily functional accessories that closed over windows to protect against damaging wind and rain. Today, shutters are mostly fixed panels that serve an ornamental purpose. Even the fasteners now feature a decorative head cover that blends in with the shutter.

Installing shutters is quick and easy, and makes a big impact on your home's appearance. They're a great way to add a splash of color to an otherwise monotone exterior.

Shutters that are larger than 55" receive six screws, one at each corner and two in the middle, while smaller shutters are fastened only in the corners. The exact location for the screws is somewhat flexible, as long as you don't get too close to the edges. For installation over vinyl siding, insert the fastener through the top, rather than the bottom, of the siding panel. For brick, fasten the screws into the mortar, rather than the brick. Drill and insert screws one at a time. If you drill all the holes first, the shutter may move slightly in the process and the holes won't line up.

Everything You Need

Tools: drill with ¼" bit, hammer.

Materials: shutters.

How to Install Shutters

1 Hold the shutter in place next to the window, centered from top to bottom. At one corner of the shutter, drill a ¼" hole, 3¼" deep through the shutter and into the wall.

2 Insert a fastener that came with the shutter into the hole. Use a hammer to gently tap the fastener until it's flush against the shutter.

TIP: *Be careful not to overtighten the fasteners or it will create a dimple in the shutter.*

3 Drill holes and insert fasteners in the remaining three corners. If the shutter requires six fasteners, drill two holes in the middle of the shutter, along the outside edges, and insert fasteners.

4 Place the second shutter on the opposite side of the window. Keep the top and bottom parallel with the first shutter by measuring down from the window. Follow steps 1 to 3 to install the second shutter.

Soffits, Gutters & Ventilation Systems

In addition to the roofing and siding systems, your home's exterior has a soffit system that connects the roofing and the siding. The soffit system is also a key component in the exterior ventilation of your home. In some cases, your home will also have a gutter system for handling water runoff from the roof. At a minimum, you should have one sq. ft. of attic ventilation, both intake and outtake, for every 300 sq. ft. of attic space.

This section details how to install soffits (air intakes) and roof vents (air outtakes). If you're planning a large exterior project that includes replacing the siding, install the soffits before the siding. Also included in this section is information on installing fascia and gutters. Fascia is installed between the roof and the soffits, and gutters are placed over the fascia.

A free-flowing gutter system directs rainwater away from your house, which protects your foundation from leaks, prevents dripping water from staining your siding, and keeps ice from forming on your walkways in the winter.

All of these projects involve working on ladders, scaffolding, or on the roof. Make sure your ladders are set securely and evenly on the ground, and move when necessary so you can work comfortably and safely.

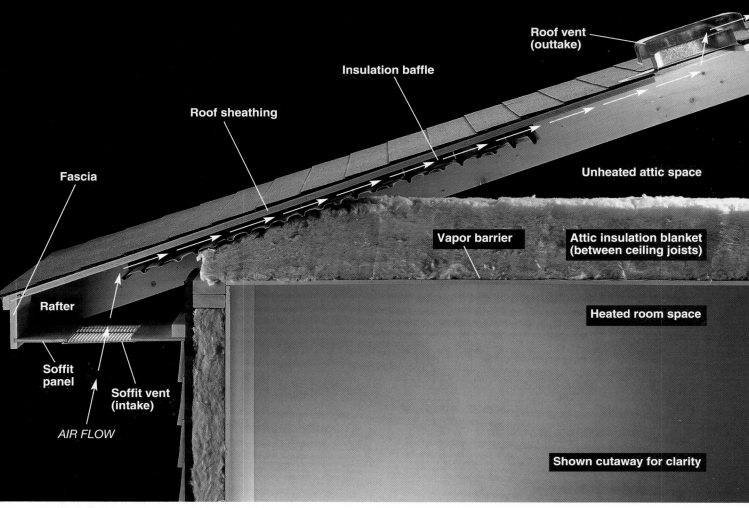

Sufficient airflow prevents heat buildup in your attic, and it helps protect your roof from damage caused by condensation or ice. A typical ventilation system has vents in the soffits to admit fresh air, which flows upward beneath the roof sheathing and exits through the roof vents.

Soffit & Roof Vents

An effective ventilation system equalizes temperatures on both sides of the roof, which helps keep your house cooler in the summer and prevents ice dams along the roof eaves in cold climates.

One strategy for increasing roof ventilation is to add more of the existing types of vents. Or, if you're reroofing, consider replacing all of your roof vents with a continuous ridge vent (pages 188 to 189). You can increase intake ventilation by adding more soffit vents. If you're replacing your soffits with aluminum soffits, install vented soffit panels that allow air intake (pages 180 to 183).

Determining Ventilation Requirements

Measure attic floor space to determine how much ventilation you need. You should have one sq. ft. each of intake and outtake ventilation for every 300 square feet of unheated attic floor space.

Soffit vents can be added to increase airflow into attics on houses with a closed soffit system.

Continuous soffit vents provide even airflow into attics. They are usually installed during new construction, but they can be added as retrofits to unvented soffit panels.

Roof vents can be added near the ridge line when you need to increase outtake ventilation. Fixed roof vents are easy to install and have no mechanical parts that can break down.

Vented soffit panels are used with aluminum soffits to allow airflow along the eaves.

Gable and dormer vents generally are installed to increase ventilation. The vents come in a variety of styles and colors to match the siding.

Continuous ridge vents create an even outtake airflow because they span the entire ridge. Barely noticeable from the ground, ridge vents can be added at any time.

Tools & Materials

The tools and materials needed for soffits, fascia, gutters, and vents are tools and materials that you probably already own. Very few specialty tools are needed, and even then, they're fairly inexpensive. The photos on these two pages show the complete list of tools you'll need.

Tools for soffits and fascia include: circular saw (A), cordless drill (B), jig saw (C), aviation snips (D), level (E), hammer (F), tape measure (G), caulk gun (H), chalk line (I), pry bar (J), and framing square (K).

Tools for gutters include: cordless drill (A), rotary saw (B), caulk gun (C), hacksaw (D), chalk line (E), aviation snips (F), hammer (G), tape measure (H), and rivet gun and rivets (I).

Caulks for gutters, soffits, and vents include (from left): Polyurethane sealant with elasticity for joints that require movement, elastomeric latex sealant for joints that require flexibility and will be painted, silicone caulk for joints exposed to water that won't get painted, and roofing cement for roofing projects.

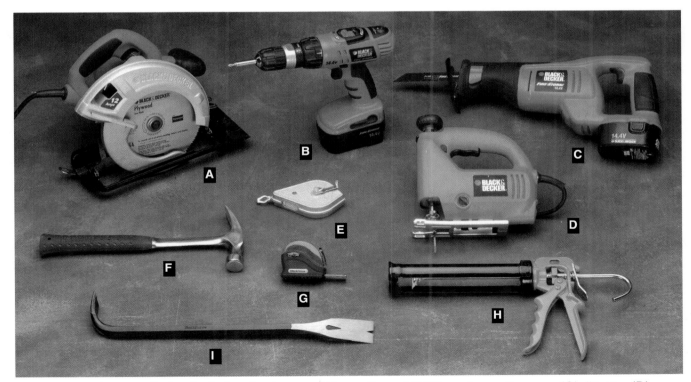

Tools for roofing ventilation include: circular saw (A), cordless drill (B), reciprocating saw (C), jig saw (D), chalk line (E), hammer (F), tape measure (G), caulk gun (H), and pry bar (I).

179

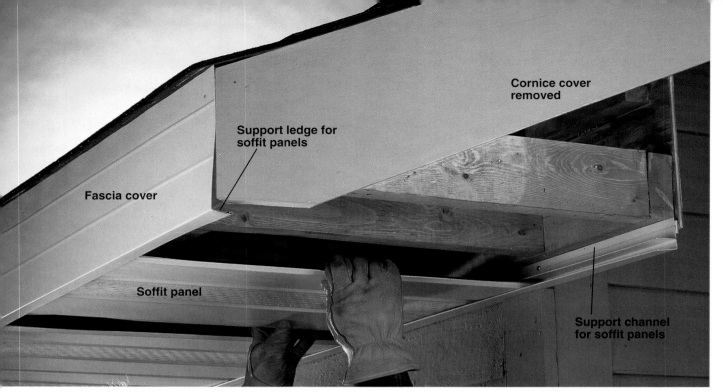

Cornice cover removed

Support ledge for soffit panels

Fascia cover

Soffit panel

Support channel for soffit panels

Install a new soffit system if your old system has failed, or if pests have infested the open eaves areas of your roof overhang. A complete soffit system consists of fabricated fascia covers, soffit panels (nonventilated or ventilated), and support channels that hold the panels at the sides of your house. Most soffit systems sold at building centers are made of aluminum.

Installing Aluminum Soffits

Older soffits may be weathered or rotted, and may not allow adequate airflow. If more than 15 percent of your soffits need to be repaired, your best option is to replace them. This project shows how to completely remove the old soffits and fascia, and install aluminum soffits, which are maintenance free. If your old subfascia is in good condition, it will not need to be replaced.

The project starting on the opposite page details the installation of soffits on an eaves system that has rafter lookouts. The soffits are installed directly beneath these lookouts. If your eaves do not have rafter lookouts, follow the instructions starting on page 182. This project also shows how to install soffits around corners.

For both eaves systems, an F-channel serves as a mounting channel to hold the soffits in place along the house. You can also install the channel along the subfascia, as shown in step 4 on page 181, or you can nail the soffits directly to the subfascia, as shown in step 4 on page 183. Drive nail heads flush with the surface. Driving the nails too deep can knock the soffits out of shape and prevent movement. Since the soffits will receive addition nailing when the fascia is installed, you don't need to drive a nail in every

V-groove in the soffits.

To cut soffits, use a circular saw with a fine-tooth blade installed backward. Don't cut all of your panels at the start of the job since the width will probably change slightly as you move across the house.

Use vented soffit panels to work in conjunction with roof or attic vents. This improves airflow underneath the roof, which prevents moisture damage and ice dams. Provide one sq. ft. of soffit vents for every 150 sq. ft. of unheated attic space. For a consistent appearance, make sure all of the fins on the soffit vents are pointed in the same direction.

Everything You Need

Tools: flat pry bar, hammer, circular saw with fine-tooth metal blade (installed backward), drill, tape measure, aviation snips, level, framing square.

Materials: soffit panels, F-channel (mounting channel), T-channel, 1¼" aluminum trim nails, 16d common nails, nailing strips, drip edge, 2¼" deck screws, 8d box nails, 2 × 4, 1 × 8 or 2 × 8 subfascia (if needed).

How to Install Aluminum Soffits (with Rafter Lookouts)

1 Remove trim, soffits, and fascia along the eaves, using a flat pry bar. If the eaves contain debris, such as bird nests or rotted wood, clean them out.

2 Check the rafters and rafter lookouts for decay or damage. Repair or replace them as needed.

3 Install new 1 × 8 or 2 × 8 subfascia over the rafters and rafter lookouts, using 16d nails. Butt subfascia boards together at rafter or rafter lookout locations. Install drip edge at the top of the subfascia. Leave a 1/16" gap between the drip edge and the subfascia for the fascia to fit.

4 Install F-channels for the soffit panels along the bottom inside edge of the subfascia and along the outside wall of the house, directly below the rafter lookouts. If more than one piece of channel is needed, butt pieces together.

(continued next page)

How to Install Aluminum Soffits (continued)

5 If the soffit panels will span more than 16", or if your house is subjected to high winds, add nailing strips to provide additional support.

6 Measure the distance between the mounting channels, subtract ⅛", and cut soffits to size. Slide the soffit panels in place, fitting the ends inside the mounting channels. Nail the panels to the nailing strips, if you've installed them.

7 Install soffit panels in the remaining spaces, cutting them to fit as needed. When finished, install the fascia (pages 184 to 185).

How to Install Aluminum Soffits (without Rafter Lookouts)

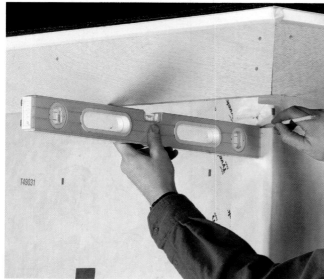

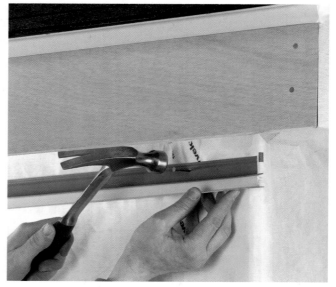

1 Remove the old soffits and fascia, following step 1 on page 181. Place a level at the bottom of the subfascia board, level across to the house, and make a mark. Measure down from the mark a distance equal to the thickness of the soffits (usually about ¼"). Do this on each end of the wall. Snap a chalk line between the lower marks.

2 Start the F-channel at a corner and align the bottom edge with the chalk line. Nail the channel to the wall at stud locations, using 8d box nails. If more than one F-channel is needed, butt the pieces together.

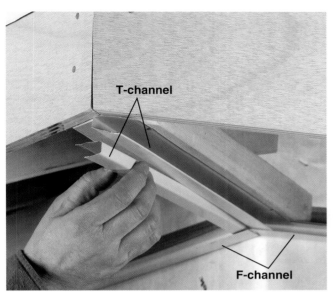

T-channel

F-channel

3 At corners, cut a 2 × 4 to fit between the house and the inside corner of the subfascia to provide support for the T-channel. Notch the 2 × 4 as needed, then nail in place so when the T-channel is installed, it will be aligned with the F-channel. Cut the T-channel to fit. Place it against the 2 × 4, setting the back edge inside the F-channel, and nail in place.

DuPor

4 Measure between the F-channel and the outside edge of the subfascia. Subtract ¼" and cut the soffits to size. For corners, miter the panels to fit the T-channel. Install the first panel inside the channel. Make sure the panel is square to the subfascia, using a framing square. Nail the panel to the subfascia at the V-grooves. Slide the next panel against the first, locking them together. Nail the panel in place. Install remaining panels the same way.

Variations for Installing Aluminum Soffits

Straight corners are made by installing the T-channel parallel with one of the F-channels. Align the outside edge of the T-channel with the outside edge of the installed F-channel. Keep the T-channel back ¼" from the outside of the subfascia, and nail it in place. Install the soffits in the channels.

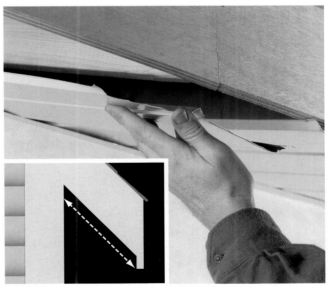

Inclined overhangs allow soffits to run the same angle as the rafters. At the end of the rafter overhangs, measure from the bottom of the rafter to the bottom of the subfascia. Add the thickness of the soffits, then measure down from the rafters along the wall and make a mark at this distance. Do this on each end of the wall. Snap a chalk line between the marks. Align the bottom of the F-channel with the chalk line, nail the channel to the wall, then install the soffits.

The fascia is installed over the subfascia to cover the exposed edges of the soffits and enhance the appearance of your home. The fascia is usually the same color and material as your soffits.

Installing Aluminum Fascia

Fascia fits under the drip edge and against the subfascia to provide a smooth transition from the roof to the eaves. You may need to temporarily remove any nails in the face of the drip edge so the fascia can slide in behind it. If your roof does not have drip edge, install a finish trim, such as undersill, at the top of the subfascia to receive the fascia.

If you're also replacing your gutters, take down the gutters first, then install the fascia. If you don't want to remove the gutters, you can slip the fascia behind them while they're in place.

Fascia is nailed along the lip covering the soffits, and the top is held in place by the drip edge, so it doesn't require any face nailing.

Everything You Need

Tools: hammer, aviation snips, tape measure, chalk line.

Materials: fascia, aluminum trim nails.

How to Install Aluminum Fascia

TIP: *If your old fascia is wood and still in good shape, you can install aluminum fascia over it without removing it.*

1 Remove the old fascia, if necessary. Measure from the top of the drip edge to the bottom of the soffits, and subtract ¼". Cut the fascia to this measurement by snapping a chalk line across the face and cutting with aviation snips. (This cut edge will be covered by the drip edge.)

2 Slide the cut edge of the fascia behind the drip edge. Place the bottom lip over the soffits. Make sure the fascia is tight against the soffits and against the subfascia, then nail through the lip into the subfascia. Nail approximately every 16" at a V-groove location in the soffits.

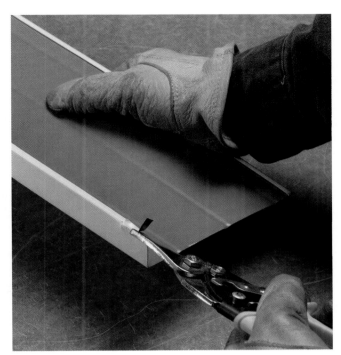

3 To overlap fascia panels, cut the ridge on the lip of the first panel 1" from the end, using aviation snips. Place the second panel over the first, overlapping the seam by 1". Nail the fascia in place.

4 At outside corners, cut the lip and top edge of the first panel 1" from the end. Place a piece of wood 1" from the end, and bend the panel to form a 90° angle. Install the panel at the corner. Cut a 45° angle in the lip of the second panel. Align the end of this panel with the corner, overlapping the first panel.

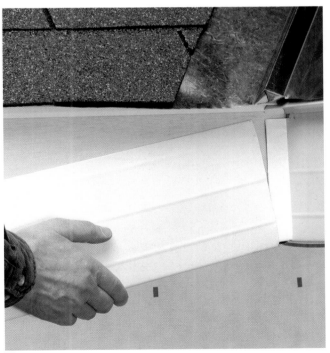

5 For inside corners, cut and bend the first panel back 1" from the end to make a tab. Install the panel. On the second panel, cut a 45° angle in the lip. Slide the panel over the first panel, butting the end against the adjacent fascia. Nail the panel in place.

Wood soffits cover the eaves area between the fascia and siding. Painted soffit moldings beneath the soffits give the house a finished look. Soffit vents installed at regular intervals play a vital role in the home's ventilation system.

Installing Wood Soffits

Wood soffits are typically used on houses with wood or fiber cement siding, and are painted the same color as the trim. To see how the soffits fit in relation to the fascia and rafters, refer to the photo on page 240. You can use plywood or engineered wood for the soffits. Engineered wood has the advantage of being treated to resist termites and fungus, and it's more resistant to warping and shrinking. Plywood has the advantage of being less expensive. If your soffits are more than 24" wide, install a nailing strip between panels to hold the seams tightly together.

When replacing soffits, you may need to remove the top course of siding and any trim pieces under the old soffits before starting the new installation. Remove the pieces carefully, then reinstall them once the soffit job is finished.

Everything You Need

Tools: hammer, circular saw, level, chalk line, caulk gun, paintbrush, drill, jig saw.

Materials: ⅜" plywood, 16d box nails, 6d corrosion-resistant nails, 2 × 2 lumber, acrylic latex caulk, vents, primer, paint.

How to Install Wood Soffits

1 Hold a level against the bottom edge of the sub-fascia and level across to make a mark on the wall. Do this on both ends of the wall, then snap a chalk line between the marks.

TIP: *The distance between the wall and subfascia may vary over the length of the house. Measure at different points for more accurate measurements.*

2 Align the bottom edge of 2 × 2 lumber with the chalk line. Nail the lumber to wall studs, using 16d nails.

3 Measure the distance from the wall to the outside of the subfascia, subtract ¼", and rip the soffits to this width. Apply primer to the soffits. If using wood that's already primed, apply primer to the cut edges only.

4 Place the soffit against the 2 × 2 and subfascia, staying ⅛" from the edges. Nail in place, using 6d nails. Install remaining soffits, keeping a ⅛" gap between panels.

5 Caulk the gaps between soffits and between the soffits and wall. Paint soffits as desired. Let the paint dry. Mark the vent locations in the soffits by holding the vent in place and tracing around it. Drill starter holes at opposite corners of the outline, then cut out the opening with a jig saw. Install the vent, using the fasteners that came with it. Do this at each vent location.

Variation. If the soffits have rafter lookouts, you don't need to install 2 × 2s. Instead, nail the soffits directly to the rafter headers and lookouts. Make sure soffit seams fall midway across rafter lookouts.

Continuous ridge vents work in conjunction with the soffits to allow airflow under the roof decking. Installed at the roof peak and covered with cap shingles, ridge vents are less conspicuous than other roof vents.

Installing a Ridge Vent

If you need attic ventilation, installing a continuous ridge vent will get the job done. Since they're installed along the entire ridge of the roof, they provide an even flow of air along the entire underside of the roof decking. Combined with continuous soffit vents, this is the most effective type of ventilation system.

Since the vents are installed along the ridge, they're practically invisible, eliminating any disruptions to the roof. Other vent types, such as roof louvers and turbines, often distract from the roof's aesthetics.

Installing one continuous ridge vent is quicker and easier than installing other types of vents that need to be placed in several locations across the roof. It also saves you from having to make numerous cuts in your finished roof, which can disturb surrounding shingles.

Everything You Need

Tools: hammer, circular saw, tape measure, chalk line, flat pry bar.

Materials: ridge vents, 1½" roofing nails.

How to Install a Ridge Vent

1 Remove the ridge caps, using a flat pry bar. Measure down from the peak the width of the manufacturer's recommended opening, and mark each end of the roof. Snap a chalk line between the marks. Repeat for the other side of the peak. Remove any nails in your path.

2 Set the blade depth of a circular saw to cut the sheathing, but not the rafters. Cut along each chalk line, staying 12" from the edges of the roof. Remove the cut sheathing, using a pry bar.

3 Measure down from the peak half the width of the ridge vent, and make a mark on both ends of the roof. Snap a line between the marks. Do this on both sides of the peak.

TIP: If a chimney extends through the peak, leave 12" of sheathing around the chimney.

4 Center the ridge vent over the peak, aligning the edges with the chalk lines. Install using roofing nails that are long enough to penetrate the roof sheathing.

5 Butt sections of ridge vents together and nail the ends. Install vents across the entire peak, including the 12" sections at each end of the roof that were not cut away.

6 Place ridge cap shingles over the ridge vents. Nail them with two 1½" roofing nails per cap. Overlap the caps as you would on a normal ridge. If the caps you removed in step 1 are still in good shape, you can reuse them. Otherwise, use new ones.

189

Installing New Vents

If you need more ventilation for your attic, but you don't want to replace your entire soffits or embark on a roofing project, you can add vents to your existing wood soffits and roof.

This project shows how to add soffit vents for air intake, and how to add roof vents for air outtake. These additional vents increase the airflow under your roof, helping to eliminate heat buildup in your attic.

Everything You Need

Tools: hammer, pry bar, chalk line, caulk gun, tape measure, drill, jig saw, utility knife, chalk line.

Materials: rubber-gasket nails, roof cement, stainless steel screws, soffit vent covers, roof vents, siliconized acrylic caulk, screwdriver.

Adding vents to wood soffits and the roof can increase airflow in the attic.

How to Install New Vents

1 Examine the eaves area from inside your attic to make sure there is nothing obstructing air flow from the soffits. If insulation is blocking the air passage, install insulation baffles.

2 Draw a cutout for the soffit vent cover on the soffit panel. Center the vents between the fascia and the side of the house. The cover outline should be ¼" smaller on all sides than the soffit vent cover.

3 Drill a starter hole, then cut the vent openings with a jig saw.

TIP: *For visual effect, install new vent covers with the louvers pointing in the same direction.*

4 Caulk the flanges of the vent cover. Screw the vent cover to the soffit.

Ridge pole

5 Mark the location for the roof vent by driving a nail through the roof sheathing. Center the nail between rafters, 16" to 24" from the ridge pole.

6 Center a vent cover over the nail on the outside of the roof. Outline the base flange of the vent cover on the shingles, then remove shingles in an area 2" inside the outline. Mark the roof vent hole, using the marker nail as a centerpoint. Cut the hole, using a reciprocating saw or jig saw.

7 Apply roof cement to the underside of the base flange. Set the vent cover in position, slipping the flange under the shingles, centered over the vent-hole cutout.

8 Secure the roof vent to the sheathing with rubber-gasket nails on all sides of the flange. Tack down any loose shingles. Do not nail through the flange when attaching shingles.

191

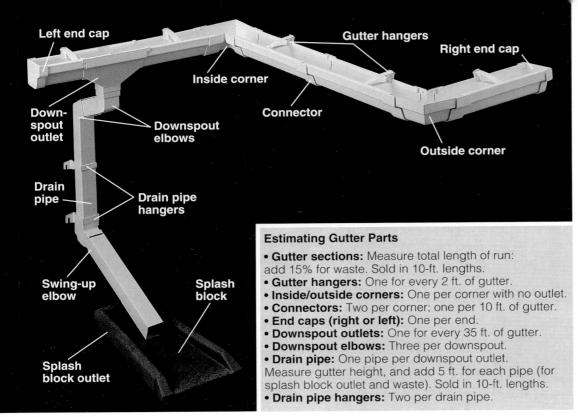

Left end cap

Gutter hangers

Right end cap

Inside corner

Connector

Downspout outlet

Downspout elbows

Outside corner

Drain pipe

Drain pipe hangers

Swing-up elbow

Splash block

Splash block outlet

Estimating Gutter Parts
- **Gutter sections:** Measure total length of run: add 15% for waste. Sold in 10-ft. lengths.
- **Gutter hangers:** One for every 2 ft. of gutter.
- **Inside/outside corners:** One per corner with no outlet.
- **Connectors:** Two per corner; one per 10 ft. of gutter.
- **End caps (right or left):** One per end.
- **Downspout outlets:** One for every 35 ft. of gutter.
- **Downspout elbows:** Three per downspout.
- **Drain pipe:** One pipe per downspout outlet. Measure gutter height, and add 5 ft. for each pipe (for splash block outlet and waste). Sold in 10-ft. lengths.
- **Drain pipe hangers:** Two per drain pipe.

Vinyl snap-together gutter systems are easy to install and relatively inexpensive, and they won't rot or deteriorate. The slip joints allow for expansion and contraction, which contribute to their reliability and longevity.

Installing Vinyl Gutters

Installing a snap-together vinyl gutter system is a manageable task for most do-it-yourselfers. Snap-together gutter systems are designed for ease of installation, requiring no fasteners other than the screws used to attach the gutter hangers to the fascia.

Before you purchase new gutters, create a detailed plan and cost estimate. Include all of the necessary parts, not just the gutter and drain pipe sections—they make up only part of the total system. Test-fit the pieces on the ground before you begin the actual installation.

Everything You Need

Tools: chalk line, tape measure, drill, hacksaw.

Materials: 1¼" deck screws, gutters, drain pipes, connectors, fittings, hangers.

How to Install Vinyl Gutters

TIP: When sloping gutters toward downspouts, have a ¼" slope for each 10 ft. of horizontal run.

1 Mark a point at the high end of each gutter run, 1" from the top of the fascia. Snap chalk lines that slope toward downspouts. For runs longer than 35 ft., mark a slope from a high point in the center toward downspouts at each end.

2 Install downspout outlets near the ends of gutter runs (at least one outlet for every 35 ft. of run). The tops of the outlets should be flush with the slope line, and they should align with end caps on the corners of the house, where drain pipes will be attached.

3 Following the slope line, attach hangers or support clips for hangers for a complete run. Attach them to the fascia at 24" intervals, using deck screws.

4 Following the slope line, attach outside and inside corners at all corner locations that don't have end caps.

5 Use a hacksaw to cut gutter sections to fit between outlets and corners. Attach the end caps and connect the gutter sections to the outlets. Cut and test-fit gutter sections to fit between outlets, allowing for expansion gaps.

6 Working on the ground, join the gutter sections together, using connectors. Attach gutter hangers to the gutter (for models with support clips mounted on the fascia). Hang the gutters, connecting them to the outlets.

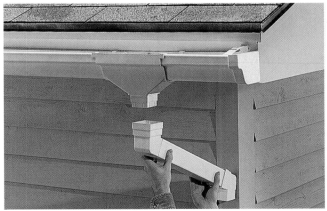

7 Cut a section of drain pipe to fit between two downspout elbows. One elbow should fit over the tail of the downspout outlet and the other should fit against the wall. Assemble the parts, slip the top elbow onto the outlet, and secure the other to the siding with a drain pipe hanger.

8 Cut a piece of drain pipe to fit between the elbow at the top of the wall and the end of the drain pipe run, staying at least 12" above the ground. Attach an elbow, and secure the pipe to the wall with a drain pipe hanger. Add accessories, such as splash blocks, to help channel water away from the house (inset).

Installing Seamless Gutters

Seamless gutters are continuous lengths of gutters, rather than two or more sections fastened together. By eliminating the seams, you eliminate the potential for leaks. However, "seamless" is a bit of a misnomer. There are still seams at the corners and ends, which need to be sealed.

The gutters should extend slightly past the edge of the fascia, aligning with the edges of the roofing. The back edge of the gutter slides behind the drip edge. When preparing the gutters, zip screws are preferred over rivets. They don't require pre-drilling, and they can be unscrewed later.

Everything You Need

Tools: tape measure, drill with ¼" hex-drive bit, caulk gun, chalk line, hammer, tin snips, hacksaw.

Materials: gutters, zip screws, gutter sealant or silicone caulk, hangers, gutter outlets, downspouts, end caps, elbows, hangers, downspout brackets, end box.

Seamless gutters are fabricated on-site, or they can be delivered to your home at the specified length.

How to Install Seamless Gutters

1 At the fascia's midpoint, measure down from the drip edge and make a mark for the bottom of the gutter. Mark both ends of the fascia, adding a ¼" slope for every 10 ft. of gutter. Snap chalk lines between the marks.

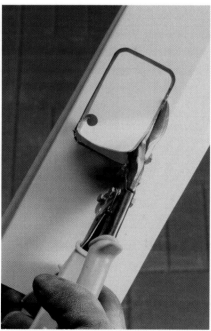

2 Mark the downspout locations on the gutter. Set a gutter outlet at each mark, centered from front to back, and trace around it. Cut out the holes, using tin snips or a rotary saw.

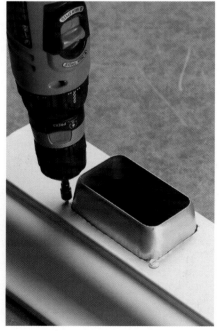

3 Apply a bead of sealant under the lip of the outlet. Place the outlet in the hole in the gutter. Press firmly in place, then attach from the bottom side of the gutter, using zip screws.

4 Place an end cap over the end of the gutter. Drive zip screws through the flange into the gutter. Apply ample sealant along the inside edges of the cap.

5 Apply a small bead of sealant on the bottom and sides inside a corner box. Slide the end of the gutter inside the box. Fasten the gutter and box together, using zip screws. Apply ample sealant along the inside seam.

6 Clip gutter hangers to the gutter every 24". Lift the gutter into place, sliding the back side under the drip edge and aligning the bottom with the chalk line. Drive the nail or screw in each hanger through the fascia to install.

TIP: Assemble the elbows and downspout so the top pieces always fit inside bottom pieces.

7 Fasten an elbow to the gutter outlet, driving a zip screw through each side. Hold another elbow in place against the house. Measure the distance between the elbows, adding 2" at each end for overlap. Cut a downspout to this length, using a hacksaw. Crimp the corners of the downspout for easy insertion and fasten together.

8 Fasten downspout brackets to the wall for the top and bottom of the downspout, and every 8 ft. in between. Cut a downspout that spans the length of the wall, and attach it to the elbow at the top. Install another elbow at the end of the downspout. Fasten the brackets to the downspout.

Installing De-icing Cables

In cold climates, successive cycles of freezing and thawing can allow ice to force its way under roof shingles, forming ice dams. These dams can result in leaky roofs and can pull gutters away from the fascia. De-icing cables prevent these problems by not allowing ice to form on the roof and gutters. Keep in mind, however, that ice dams are usually caused by inadequate attic ventilation. De-icing cables will stop ice from forming, but they won't solve your ventilation problems.

When purchasing a de-icing system, determine the length of cable you need, then buy an amount close to that length. The cables cannot be cut, but you can run excess cable along valleys and downspouts. A ground-fault circuit-interrupter (GFCI) receptacle is recommended (and may be required by code) for the power source. Keep the cables warm until they're ready to be installed. **Caution: Read manufacturer's instructions carefully. Incorrect installation can result in electrical shock, allow ice dams to form, or in a worst case scenario, cause a fire. Make sure the roof and gutters are clean prior to installation.**

Photo courtesy of Easy Heat Inc.

De-icing cables are used to prevent ice dams from forming on the roof. Cold temperatures and water running down the roof trip the sensor to turn on the unit. The cables then heat up areas along the eaves end of the roof, the gutters, and the downspouts, eliminating ice formation.

Everything You Need

Tools: tape measure, cordless drill.

Materials: de-icing kit, roof cable clips, roof cable spacers.

De-icing cables are installed on the part of the roof that's over non-heated areas of the house, which is usually the roofing above the overhang.

How to Install De-icing Cables

1 Mount the control box to the soffit, using the screws that came with the box. Choose a location that's close to an electrical outlet.

2 Secure the heating cable to the roof, using roof cable clips. Place the cable in a looping pattern, running the cable the proper length up the roof with 24" between peaks. Clip the cable at the top and bottom of each loop.

3 Extend the heating cable up the side of the valley 36", then bring it back down on the other side of the valley. Continue looping the cable across the roof.

TIP: *Wires connecting to power sources and the mounting box need a "drip loop." Hang the wires well below the connection, then run them back up again.*

4 Set the cable in the gutter. Hold it in place with cable spacers attached to the cable clips. Insert the end of the cable into the downspout.

5 Place the thermostat block and sensor wire from the control box into the gutter, within 2" of the heating cable. Drape the sensor wire over at least one gutter support strap. Clip the wire next to the cable for one loop, then extend the wire straight up the roof, at least 24", at the peak of the second loop.

Exterior Painting

Painting is a perfect project for the do-it-yourselfer—it doesn't require a big investment in specialty tools and materials, it's a project almost every homeowner can do, and it can save you a lot of money. With some care and patience, you can end up with a professional-looking finish.

Your painting project breaks naturally into two stages—preparing the surfaces, and applying the paint. Although the preparation work is more time consuming, and less glamorous, than the application, it's a critical component of a successful paint job. If you invest time preparing the surface, you'll end up with a painted finish that will look great for years to come. In fact, paint can last 10 years or more when applied correctly over a well-prepared, primed surface.

Before starting, plan your work sequence so you only tackle one side of the house at a time. It's best to finish the preparation work on one section, paint it, then move on to the next section rather than preparing the entire house first, then start painting. Once you scrape and sand the old paint, you expose your siding to the elements, which can cause the wood pores to become plugged. If you wait too long to apply the paint, it won't form a strong bond with the wood.

Conduct regular inspections to make sure the paint is holding up. Pressure wash the siding once a year to remove debris and help extend the life of the paint. If you notice signs of paint failure, take immediate steps to fix it. If you touch up minor problems, such as chips and localized flaking, you can prevent water from building up beneath the surface. If you sand, prime, and paint cracks and alligatoring as soon as they occur, you can prevent mildew formation.

Safety Warning:

Lead-based paint is a hazardous material—its handling and disposal are strictly regulated. If your home was built before 1976, test the paint for lead, using a lead testing kit (available at home improvement and paint stores). Call your local building inspector or waste management department for information on handling and disposing of lead-based paint.

Tools & Materials

High-quality painting tools, primers, and paints usually produce better results with less work than less-expensive products. The return on an investment in quality products is a project that goes smoothly and results in an attractive, durable paint job.

Plan to prime all unpainted surfaces and any surfaces or patches that have been stripped or worn down to bare wood. For bare wood, the best approach is to apply one primer coat followed by two topcoats. But if the surface was previously painted and the old paint is still good, one coat of new paint is enough.

Although removing layers of old paint can be quite a chore, the proper materials can make the task go faster. If you don't own all of the specialty tools you need, such as a siding sander and heat gun, you can rent them at some home improvement stores and most rental centers. As you plan your painting project, make a list of the tools and materials you need.

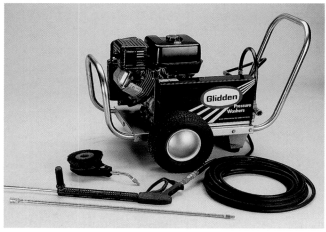

Buy or rent a pressure washer and attachments to clean siding thoroughly and remove loose, flaky paint. Make sure to get the right unit. One with less than 1200 psi won't do a good job, and one with more than 2500 psi could damage your siding.

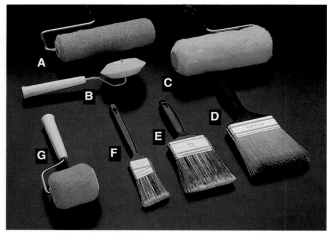

Tools for applying paint include: roller and sleeve with ⅜" nap (A), corner roller (B), roller with ⅝" nap (C), 4" paintbrush (D), 3" paintbrush (E), 2" sash brush (F), 3"-wide roller (G). Note: All brushes shown have synthetic bristles, for use with latex-based paint.

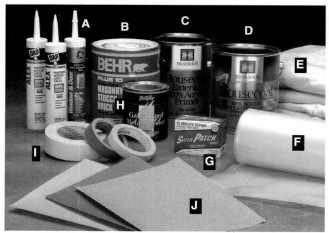

Materials for painting include: painter's caulk (A), masonry, stucco, and brick paint (B), primer (C), house paint (D), drop cloth (E), plastic sheeting (F), epoxy wood filler (G), metal primer (H), masking tape (I), and 80-, 120-, and 150-grit sandpaper (J).

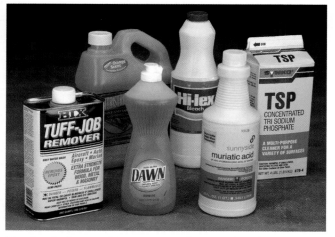

Products for surface preparation and maintenance include (from left): stripper for removing varnish, epoxy, and synthetic finishes; paint stripper for removing thick layers of paint; detergent; chlorine bleach for cleaning surfaces; muriatic acid for cleaning rust from metal; and TSP (trisodium phosphate).

Estimating Paint

To estimate the amount of paint you need for one coat:

Calculate the square footage of the walls (length × height), the square footage of the soffit panels and trim that will be painted, and add 15% waste allowance.

Subtract from this figure the square footage of doors and windows.

Check the paint coverage rate listed on the label (350 sq. ft. per gallon is average).

Divide the total square footage by the paint coverage rate to determine the number of gallons you need.

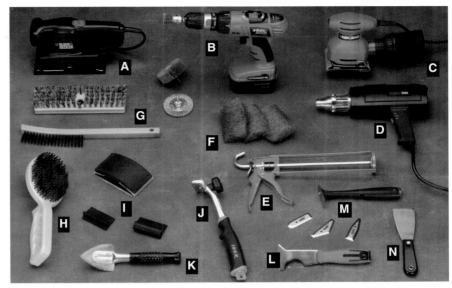

Tools for paint removal include: ⅓ sheet finish sander (A), drill with wire-wheel attachments (B), ¼ sheet palm sander (C), heat gun (D), caulk gun (E), steel wool (F), wire brushes (G), stiff-bristled brush (H), sanding blocks (I), paint scraper (J), paint zipper (K), painter's 5-in-1 tool (L), detail scraper (M), and putty knife (N).

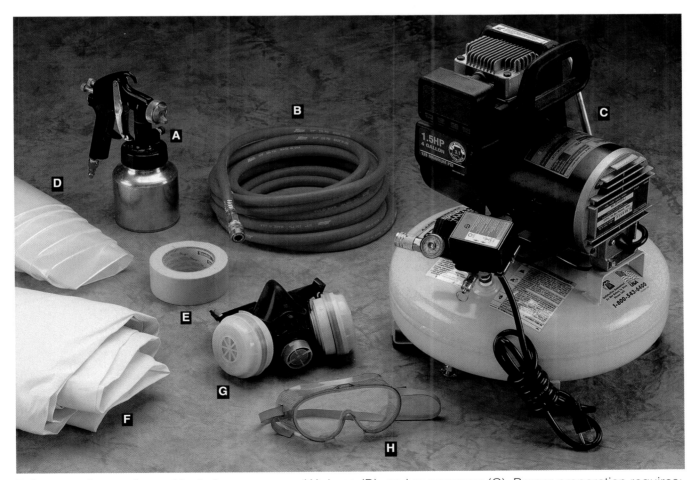

Paint-spraying equipment includes: spray gun (A), hose (B), and compressor (C). Proper preparation requires: plastic sheeting (D), masking tape (E), and drop cloths (F). Always use the necessary protective devices, including: dual-cartridge respirator (G) and safety goggles (H).

Identifying Exterior Paint Problems

Two enemies work against painted surfaces—moisture and age. A simple leak or a failed vapor barrier inside the house can ruin even the finest paint job. If you notice signs of paint failure, such as blistering or peeling, take action to correct the problem right away. If the surface damage is discovered in time, you may be able to correct it with just a little bit of touch-up painting.

Evaluating the painted surfaces of your house can help you identify problems with siding, trim, roofs, and moisture barriers. The pictures on these two pages show the most common forms of paint failure, and how to fix them. Be sure to fix any moisture problems before repainting.

Evaluate exterior painted surfaces every year, starting with areas sheltered from the sun. Paint failure will appear first in areas that receive little or no direct sunlight and is a warning sign that similar problems are developing in neighboring areas.

Common Forms of Paint Failure

Blistering appears as a bubbled surface. It results from poor preparation or hurried application of primer or paint. The blisters indicate trapped moisture is trying to force its way through the surface. To fix isolated spots, scrape and touch up. For widespread damage, remove paint down to bare wood, then apply primer and paint.

Peeling occurs when paint falls away in large flakes. It's a sign of persistent moisture problems, generally from a leak or a failed vapor barrier. If the peeling is localized, scrape and sand the damaged areas, then touch up with primer and paint. If it's widespread, remove the old paint down to bare wood, then apply primer and paint.

Alligatoring is widespread flaking and cracking, typically seen on surfaces that have many built-up paint layers. It can also be caused by inadequate surface preparation or by allowing too little drying time between coats of primer and paint. Remove the old paint, then prime and repaint.

Localized blistering and peeling indicates that moisture, usually from a leaky roof, gutter system, or interior pipe, is trapped under the paint. Find and eliminate the leak, then scrape, prime, and repaint the area.

Clearly defined blistering and peeling occurs when a humid room has an insufficient vapor barrier. If there's a clear line where an interior wall ends, remove the siding and replace the vapor barrier.

Mildew forms in cracks and in humid areas that receive little direct sunlight. Wash mildewed areas with a 1:1 solution of household chlorine bleach and water, or with trisodium phosphate (TSP).

Rust occurs when moisture penetrates paint on iron or steel. Remove the rust and loose paint with a drill and wire brush attachment, then prime and repaint.

Bleeding spots occur when nails in siding begin to rust. Remove the nails, sand out the rust, then drive in galvanized ring-shank nails. Apply metal primer, then paint to blend in with the siding.

Efflorescence occurs in masonry when minerals leech through the surface, forming a crystalline or powdery layer. Use a scrub brush and a muriatic acid solution to remove efflorescence before priming and painting.

Sanded to bare wood

Scraped and spot-sanded

Pressure-washed only

The amount of surface preparation you do will largely determine the final appearance of your paint job. Decide how much sanding and scraping you're willing to do to obtain a finish you'll be happy with.

Preparing to Paint

The key to an even paint job is to work on a smooth, clean, dry surface—so preparing the surface is essential. Generally, the more preparation work you do, the smoother the final finish will be and the longer it will last.

For the smoothest finish, sand all the way down to the bare wood with a power sander. For a less time-consuming (but rougher) finish, scrape off any loose paint, then spot-sand rough areas. You can use pressure washing to remove some of the flaking paint, but by itself, pressure washing won't create a smooth surface for painting.

Everything You Need

Tools: pressure washer, scraper, sander, sanding block, putty knife, stiff-bristled brush, wire brush, steel wool, coarse abrasive pad, drill, wire-wheel attachment, caulk gun, heat gun, proper respiratory protection.

Materials: 80-, 120-, and 150-grit sandpaper, putty, paintable siliconized caulk, muriatic acid, sealant.

How to Remove Paint

CAUTION: *Cavities behind work surfaces, particularly in soffit areas, may contain flammable debris. Cracks and open joints may allow highly heated air into these areas resulting in fire. Check them first!*

1 Use a heat gun to loosen thick layers of old paint. Aim the gun at the surface, warm the paint until it starts to bubble, then scrape the paint as soon as it releases.

2 To remove large areas of paint on wood lap siding, use a siding sander with a disk that's as wide as the reveal on your siding.

How to Prepare Surfaces for Paint

1 Clean the surface and remove loose paint by pressure washing the house. As you work, direct the water stream downward, and don't get too close to the surface with the sprayer head. Allow all surfaces to dry thoroughly before continuing.

2 Scrape off loose paint, using a paint scraper. Be careful not to damage the surface by scraping too hard.

TIP: *You can make sanding blocks from dowels, wood scraps, or garden hoses.*

3 Smooth out rough paint with a finishing sander and 80-grit sandpaper. Use sanding blocks and 80- to 120-grit sandpaper to sand hard-to-reach areas of trim.

4 Use detail scrapers to remove loose paint in hard-to-reach areas. Some of these scrapers have interchangeable heads that match common trim profiles.

5 Inspect all surfaces for cracks, rot, and other damage. Mark affected areas with colored push pins or tape. Fill the holes and cracks with epoxy wood filler.

6 Use a finishing sander with 120-grit sandpaper to sand down repaired areas, ridges, and hard edges left from the scraping process, creating a smooth surface.

How to Prepare Trim Surfaces for Paint

1 Scuff-sand glossy surfaces on doors, window casings, and all surfaces painted with enamel paint. Use a coarse abrasive pad or 150-grit sandpaper.

2 Fill cracks in siding and gaps around window and door trim with paintable siliconized acrylic caulk.

How to Remove Clear Finishes

1 Pressure-wash stained or unpainted surfaces that have been treated with a wood preservative or protectant before recoating them with fresh sealant.

2 Use a stiff-bristled brush to dislodge any flakes of loosened surface coating that weren't removed by pressure washing. Don't use a wire brush on wood surfaces.

How to Prepare Metal & Masonry for Paint

1 Remove rust and loose paint from metal hardware, such as railings and ornate trim, using a wire brush. Cover the surface with metal primer immediately after brushing to prevent the formation of new rust.

2 Scuff-sand metal siding and trim with medium-coarse steel wool or a coarse abrasive pad. Wash the surface and let dry before priming and painting.

3 Remove loose mortar, mineral deposits, or paint from mortar lines in masonry surfaces with a drill and wire-wheel attachment. Clean broad, flat masonry surfaces with a wire brush. Correct any minor damage before repainting.

4 Dissolve rust on metal hardware with diluted muriatic acid solution. When working with muriatic acid, it's important to wear safety equipment, work in a well-ventilated area, and follow all manufacturer's directions and precautions.

Applying Paint & Primer

Schedule priming and painting tasks so that you can paint within two weeks of priming surfaces. If more than two weeks pass, wash the surface with soap and water before applying the next coat.

Check the weather forecast and keep an eye on the sky while you work. Damp weather or rain within two hours of application will ruin a paint job. Don't paint when the temperature is below 50° or above 90°F. Avoid painting on windy days—it's dangerous to be on a ladder in high winds, and wind blows dirt onto the fresh paint.

Plan each day's work so you can follow the shade. Prepare, prime, and paint one face of the house at a time, and follow a logical painting order. Work from the top of the house down to the foundation, covering an entire section before you move the ladder or scaffolding.

Everything You Need

Tools: 4" paintbrush, 2½" or 3" paintbrush, sash brush, scaffolding, ladders.

Materials: primer, house paint, trim paint, cleanup materials.

Paint in a logical order, starting from the top and working your way down. Cover as much surface as you can reach comfortably without moving your ladder or scaffolding. After the paint or primer dries, touch up any unpainted areas that were covered by the ladder or ladder stabilizer.

Tips for Applying Primer & Paint

Use the right primer and paint for each job. Always read the manufacturer's recommendations.

Plan your painting sequence so you paint the walls, doors, and trim before painting stairs and porch floors. This prevents the need to touch up spills.

Apply primer and paint in the shade or indirect sunlight. Direct sun can dry primers and paints too quickly and trap moisture below the surface, which leads to blistering and peeling.

Tips for Selecting Brushes & Rollers

TIP: *It's good to keep a variety of clean brushes on hand, including 2½", 3", and 4" flat brushes, 2" and 3" trim brushes, and tapered sash brushes.*

Wall brushes, which are thick, square brushes 3" to 5" wide, are designed to carry a lot of paint and distribute it widely.

Trim and tapered sash brushes, which are 2" to 3" wide, are good for painting doors and trim, and for cutting-in small areas.

Paint rollers work best for quickly painting smooth surfaces. Use an 8" or 9" roller sleeve for broad surfaces.

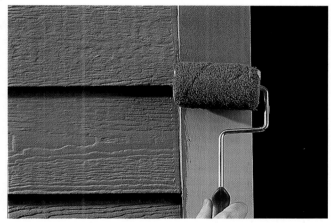

Use a 3" roller to paint flat-surfaced trim, such as end caps and corner trim.

Tips for Loading & Distributing Paint

Load your brush with the right amount of paint for the area you're covering. Use a full load of paint for broad areas, a moderate load for smaller areas and feathering strokes, and a light load when painting or working around trim.

Hold the brush at a 45° angle and apply just enough downward pressure to flex the bristles and squeeze the paint from the brush.

How to Use a Paintbrush

TIP: *Paint color can vary from one can to the next. To avoid problems, pour all of your paint into one large container and mix it thoroughly. Pour the mixed paint back into the individual cans and seal them carefully. Stir each can before use.*

1 Load the brush with a full load of paint. Starting at one end of the surface, make a long, smooth stroke until the paint begins to feather out.

2 At the end of the stroke, lift the brush without leaving a definite ending point. If the paint appears uneven or contains heavy brush marks, smooth it out without over-brushing.

3 Reload the brush and make a stroke from the opposite direction, painting over the feathered end of the first stroke to create a smooth, even surface. If the junction of the two strokes is visible, rebrush with a light coat of paint. Feather out the starting point of the second stroke.

Tips for Using Paint Rollers

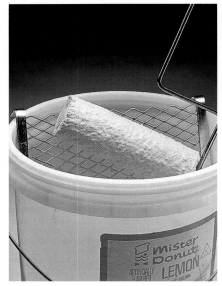

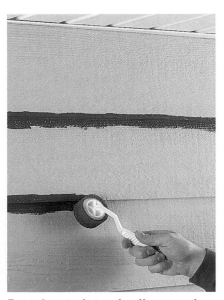

Wet the roller nap, then squeeze out the excess water. Position a roller screen inside a five-gallon bucket. Dip the roller into the paint, then roll it back and forth across the roller screen. The roller sleeve should be full, but not dripping, when lifted from the bucket.

Cone-shaped rollers work well for painting the joints between intersecting surfaces.

Doughnut-shaped rollers work well for painting the edges of lap siding and moldings.

Tips for Cleaning Painting Tools

Scrape paint from roller covers with the curved side of a cleaner tool.

Use a spinner tool to remove paint and solvent from brushes and roller covers.

Comb brushes with the spiked side of a cleaner tool to properly align bristles for drying.

How to Paint Fascia, Soffits & Trim

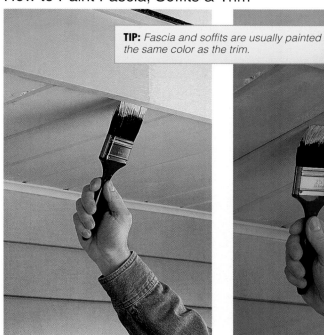

TIP: *Fascia and soffits are usually painted the same color as the trim.*

1 Prime all surfaces to be painted, and allow ample drying time. Paint the face of the fascia first, then cut in paint at the bottom edges of the soffit panels.

2 Paint the soffit panels and trim with a 4" brush. Start by cutting in around the edges of the panels, using the narrow edge of the brush, then feather in the broad surfaces of the soffit panels with full loads of paint. Be sure to get good coverage in the grooves.

3 Paint any decorative trim near the top of the house at the same time you paint the soffits and fascia. Use a 2½" or 3" paintbrush for broader surfaces, and a sash brush for more intricate trim areas.

How to Paint Siding

1 Paint the bottom edges of lap siding by holding the paintbrush flat against the wall. Paint the bottom edges of several siding pieces before returning to paint the faces of the same boards.

2 Paint the broad faces of the siding boards with a 4" brush, using the painting technique shown on page 210. Working down from the top of the house, paint as much surface as you can reach without leaning beyond the sides of the ladder.

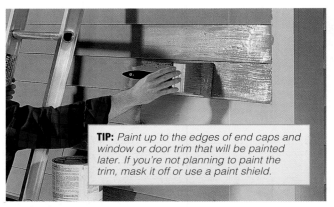

TIP: *Paint up to the edges of end caps and window or door trim that will be painted later. If you're not planning to paint the trim, mask it off or use a paint shield.*

3 Paint the siding all the way down to the foundation, working from top to bottom. Shift the ladder or scaffolding, then paint the next section.

4 On board and batten or vertical panel siding, paint the edges of the battens, or top boards, first. Paint the faces of the battens before the sides dry, then use a roller with a ⅝"-nap sleeve to paint the large, broad surfaces between the battens.

How to Paint Stucco Walls

1 Using a large paintbrush, paint the foundation with anti-chalking masonry primer, and let it dry. Using concrete paint and a 4" brush, cut in the areas around basement windows and doors.

2 Apply concrete paint to board surfaces with a paint roller and a ⅝"-nap sleeve. Use a 3" trim roller or a 3" paintbrush for trim.

How to Paint Doors, Windows & Trim

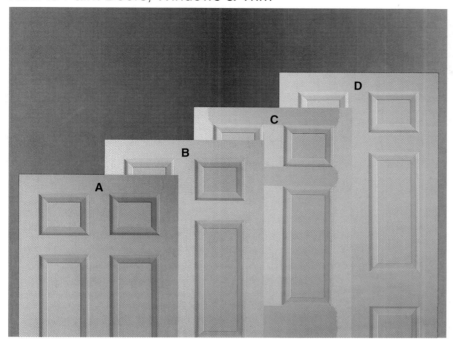

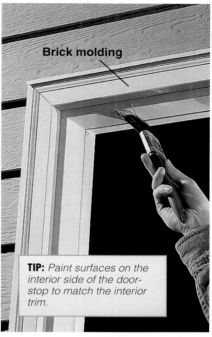

Brick molding

> **TIP:** *Paint surfaces on the interior side of the door-stop to match the interior trim.*

1 Using a sash brush, paint doors in this sequence: beveled edges of raised door panels (A), panel faces (B), horizontal rails (C), and vertical stiles (D).

2 For trim, use a trim brush or sash brush and a moderate load of paint to paint the inside edges of door and window jambs, casings, and brick molding.

3 Mask off the siding—if freshly painted, make sure it's completely dry first. Paint the outside edges of casings and brick molding. Work paint all the way into the corners created by the siding's profile.

4 Paint the faces of door jambs, casings, and brick molding, feathering fresh paint around the previously painted edges.

5 Paint wood door thresholds and porch floors with specially formulated enamel floor paint.

Paint sprayers allow you to cover large areas of siding and trim in a short amount of time. They also make it easier to paint areas that are hard to reach with a brush or roller.

Using Paint-spraying Equipment

Spray equipment can make quick work of painting, but it still requires the same careful preparation work as traditional brush and roller methods. Part of that prep work involves using plastic to completely cover doors, windows, and other areas that you don't want painted, rather than just taping them off.

Spray equipment can be purchased or rented at hardware and home improvement stores. There are several types and sizes of spray equipment, including high-volume low-pressure (HVLP), airless, air-assisted airless, and electrostatic enhanced. They all work the same way—by atomizing paint and directing it to a worksurface in a spray or fan pattern. For our project, we used an HVLP sprayer, which we recommend because it produces less overspray and more efficient paint application than other sprayers.

Be sure to read and follow all safety precautions for the spray equipment. Since the paint is under a lot of pressure, it can not only tear the skin, but it can inject toxins into the blood stream if used incorrectly. Wear the proper safety protection, such as safety glasses and a respirator, when spray painting the house.

As with other paint applications, pay close attention to the weather. Don't spray if rain is likely, and don't spray on windy days, since the wind can carry the paint particles away from the siding.

Everything You Need

Tools: utility knife, spray equipment.

Materials: paint, safety glasses, respirator, masking tape, plastic, cardboard, cheesecloth, 5-gallon bucket.

How to Paint Using a Paint Sprayer

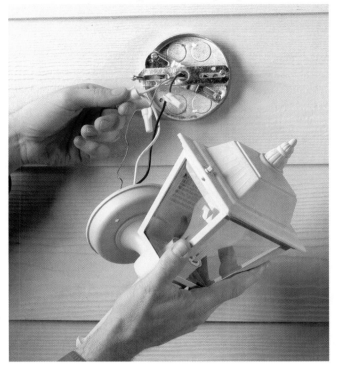

1 Remove outside light fixtures, window and door screens, and other detachable items that you don't want painted. Turn off power before disconnecting power to fixture.

2 Cover doors, windows, and any other areas you don't want painted, using plastic and masking tape.

3 Strain the paint through cheese cloth to remove particles and debris. Mix the paint together in a 5-gallon bucket. Fill the sprayer container.

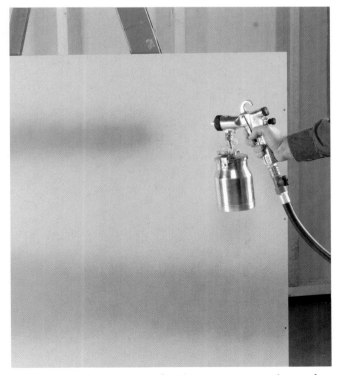

4 Spray a test pattern of paint on a scrap piece of cardboard. Adjust the pressure until you reach an even "fan" without any thick lines along the edge of the spray pattern.

(continued next page)

5 Cut-in around doors and windows with the paint. Spray the paint along each side of the doors and windows, applying the paint evenly.

6 If you happen to spray an excessive amount of paint in an area and it starts to run, stop the sprayer. Use a paintbrush to spread out the paint and eliminate the runs.

7 Hold the spray gun perpendicular to the house, approximately 12" from the wall. Start painting near the top of the wall, close to a corner. Move your entire arm, rather than just the wrist, in a steady, side-to-side motion. Do not wave your arm in an arc. Start your arm movement, then start the gun.

8 Spray the paint in an even motion, being careful not to tilt the gun. As you sweep your arm back and forth, overlap each coat of paint by 20 to 30 percent, working your way down the wall. When stopping, release the trigger before discontinuing your motion.

How to Paint Doors Using a Paint Sprayer

1 Remove the door by taking off the hinges. Remove all hardware from the door, such as handles and locks. If the door contains glass, you can either tape it off, or allow paint to get on the glass and then scrape it off with a razor after it's dry.

2 Prop up the door so it stands vertically. Starting at the top of the door, spray on the paint. As you make passes across the door, slightly go past the edges before sweeping back in the opposite direction. Wait until the paint is completely dry, then turn the door around and paint the other side.

Staining Siding

Stain lends color to wood siding, but because it is partially transparent, it also allows the natural beauty of the wood grain to show through. Water-based stains are applied with an acrylic or synthetic brush. Oil-based stains are usually applied with a natural-bristle brush.

Work in small sections at a time. Complete an entire length of board without stopping in the middle. Unlike paint, stain can darken or leave streaks if you go back over an area after it dries. Save the trim until the end, then stain it separately to get an even coverage.

Staining requires the same careful preparation work as painting. The surface must be clean and dry. Avoid working in direct sunlight so the stain doesn't dry too quickly. Check manufacturer's recommendations before staining. Some stains cannot be applied in temperatures below 50°F.

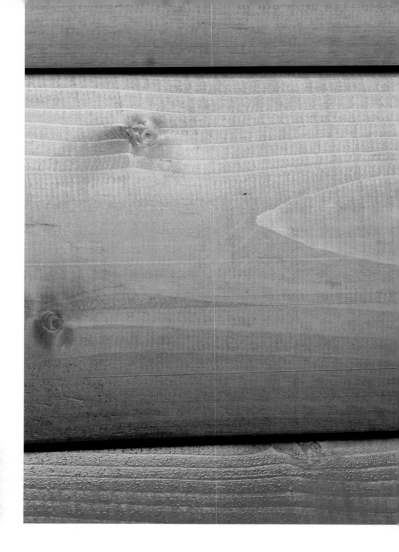

Everything You Need

Tools: paintbrush or foam brush, cloths.

Materials: stain.

How to Stain Log Cabin Siding

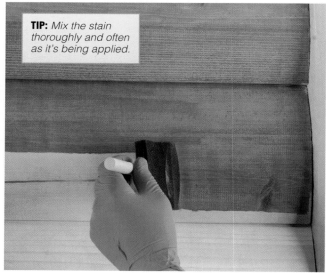

TIP: Mix the stain thoroughly and often as it's being applied.

1 Load the brush with stain. Starting at a corner, move the brush across the siding with a long, smooth stroke. Cover the entire width of the log with stain, reloading the brush as needed, applying stain in the same direction.

2 Wipe away excess stain with a clean cloth. Keep applying stain until you reach the opposite corner or an edge. Once the top course is stained, go back to the corner and start on the next row of siding, using the same technique. If the run of siding is short, such as between windows, apply stain to two rows at a time. Stain remaining courses the same way.

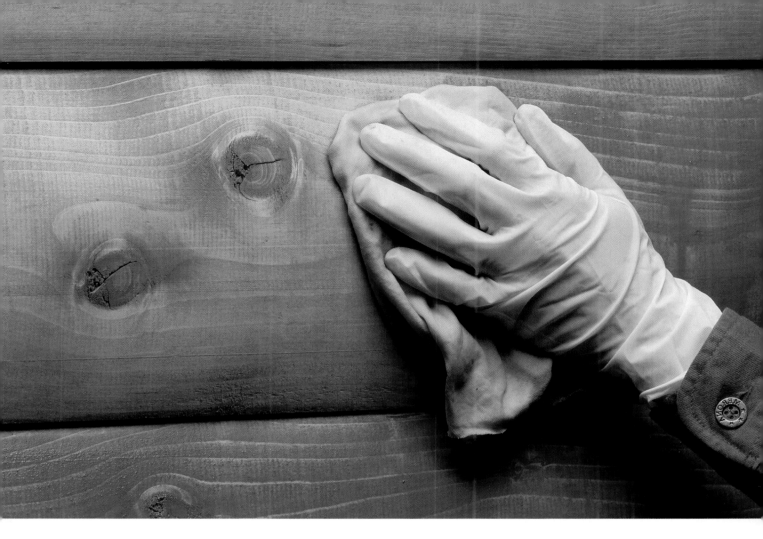

How to Stain Shingle Siding

1 Load the brush with stain. Starting at the top of a wall by a corner, apply stain to the shingles, using smooth, downward strokes. Wipe off excess stain with a cloth. Cover the face of the shingle and stain the bottom edge before moving on to the next one. Apply stain to one or two courses at a time, moving across the wall as you go. Never stop in the middle of a shingle. When you reach the opposite corner, start over on the next set of shingles. Stain remaining rows the same way.

2 Once all of the shingles are stained, apply stain to the trim. Move the brush in the same direction as the wood grain, then wipe away excess with a cloth.

Repairing Roofs & Siding

No matter how much roofing and siding materials have improved, they still need occasional repairs. The good news is that most repairs can be done relatively inexpensively, in a short amount of time, and by do-it-yourselfers. For example, wood lap siding can be repaired easily with epoxy wood filler, and roofing cement goes a long way toward patching roofs and gutters.

Before making any repairs, it's important to identify the cause of the problem so it doesn't repeat itself. If the problem is missing pieces of roofing or siding, it's a simple matter to replace them. If the problem is the result of water damage, you'll need to identify the source of the leak and fix it before going forward with the repair.

It's a good idea to perform semi-annual inspections of your roofing and siding, and look for signs of damage. It's always better to make the repairs while the repairs are still small and inexpensive to fix.

Ice dams above entries pose a danger to everyone entering and leaving the house. To permanently solve ice damming problems, like the one shown here, improve roof ventilation to reduce attic temperatures.

Inspecting & Repairing a Roof

A roof system is composed of several elements that work together to provide three basic, essential functions for your home: shelter, drainage, and ventilation. The roof covering and flashing are designed to shed water, directing it to gutters and downspouts. Air intake and outtake vents keep fresh air circulating below the roof sheathing, preventing moisture and heat buildup.

When your roof system develops problems that compromise its ability to protect your home—cracked shingles, incomplete ventilation, or damaged flashing—the damage quickly spreads to other parts of your house. Routine inspections are the best way to make sure the roof continues to do its job effectively.

Everything You Need

Tools: tape measure, wire brush, aviation snips, trowel, flat pry bar, hammer, utility knife, caulk gun.

Materials: replacement flashing, replacement shingles, roofing cement, roofing nails, plywood, double-headed nails, rubber-gasket nails.

Tips for Identifying Roofing Problems

Ice dams occur when melting snow refreezes near the eaves, causing ice to back up under the shingles, where it melts onto the sheathing and seeps into the house.

Inspect both the interior and the exterior of the roof to spot problems. From inside the attic, check the rafters and sheathing for signs of water damage. Symptoms will appear in the form of streaking or discoloration. A moist or wet area also signals water damage.

Common Roofing Problems

Wind, weather, and flying debris can damage shingles. The areas along valleys and ridges tend to take the most weather-related abuse. Torn, loose, or cracked shingles are common in these areas.

Buckled and cupped shingles are usually caused by moisture beneath the shingles. Loosened areas create an entry point for moisture and leave shingles vulnerable to wind damage.

A sagging ridge might be caused by the weight of too many roofing layers. It might also be the result of a more significant problem, such as a rotting ridge board or insufficient support for the ridge board.

Dirt and debris attract moisture and decay, which shorten a roof's life. To protect shingles, carefully wash the roof once a year, using a pressure washer. Pay particular attention to areas where moss and mildew may accumulate.

In damp climates, it's a good idea to nail a zinc strip along the center ridge of a roof, under the ridge caps. Minute quantities of zinc wash down the roof each time it rains, killing moss and mildew.

Overhanging tree limbs drop debris and provide shade that encourages moss and mildew. To reduce chances of decay, trim any limbs that overhang the roof.

How to Locate & Evaluate Leaks

1 If you have an unfinished attic, examine the underside of your roof with a flashlight on a rainy day. If you find wetness, discoloration, or other signs of moisture, trace the trail up to where the water is making its entrance.

2 Water that flows toward a wall can be temporarily diverted to minimize damage. Nail a small block of wood in the path of the water, and place a bucket underneath to catch the drip. On a dry day, drive a nail through the underside of the roof decking to mark the hole.

3 If the leak is finding its way to a finished ceiling, take steps to minimize damage until the leak can be repaired. As soon as possible, reduce the accumulation of water behind a ceiling by poking a small hole in the wallboard or plaster and draining the water.

4 Once you mark the source of a leak from inside, measure from that spot to a point that will be visible and identifiable from outside the house, such as a chimney, vent pipe, or the peak of the roof. Get up on the roof and use that measurement to locate the leak.

How to Make Emergency Repairs

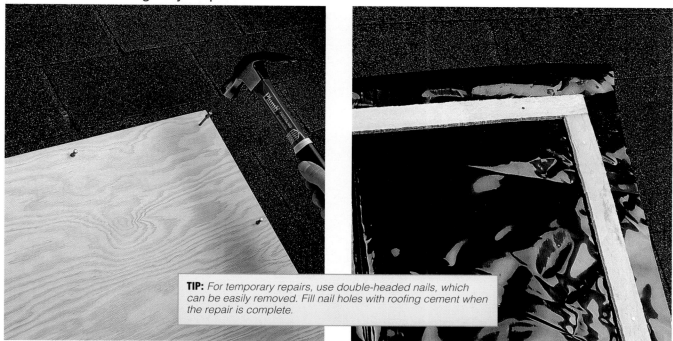

TIP: *For temporary repairs, use double-headed nails, which can be easily removed. Fill nail holes with roofing cement when the repair is complete.*

If your roof is severely damaged, the primary goal is to prevent additional damage until permanent repairs are made. Nail a sheet of plywood to the roof to serve as emergency cover to keep out the wind and water.

Cover the damaged area by nailing strips of lath around the edges of a plastic sheet or tarp.

How to Make Spot Repairs with Roofing Cement

TIP: *Heat softens the roof's surface, and cold makes it brittle. If needed, warm shingles slightly with a hair dryer to make them easier to work with and less likely to crack.*

1 To reattach a loose shingle, wipe down the felt paper and the underside of the shingle. Let each dry, then apply a liberal coat of roofing cement. Press the shingle down to seat it in the bed of cement.

2 Tack down buckled shingles by cleaning below the buckled area. Fill the area with roofing cement, then press the shingle into the cement. Patch cracks and splits in shingles with roofing cement.

3 Check the joints around flashing, which are common places for roof leaks to occur. Seal any gaps by cleaning out and replacing any failed roofing cement.

How to Replace Asphalt Shingles

1 Pull out damaged shingles, starting with the uppermost shingle in the damaged area. Be careful not to damage surrounding shingles that still are in good condition.

2 Remove old nails in and above the repair area, using a flat pry bar. Patch damaged felt paper with roofing cement.

3 Install the replacement shingles, beginning with the lowest shingle in the repair area. Nail above the tab slots, using 7/8" or 1" roofing nails.

4 Install all but the top shingle with nails, then apply roofing cement to the underside of the top shingle, above the seal line.

5 Slip the last shingle into place, under the overlapping shingle. Lift the shingles immediately above the repair area, and nail the top replacement shingle.

How to Replace Wood Shakes & Shingles

1 To age new shakes and shingles so they match existing ones, dissolve 1 pound of baking soda in 1 gallon of water. Brush the solution onto the shakes or shingles, then place them in direct sunlight for four to five hours. Rinse them thoroughly and let dry. Repeat this process until the color closely matches the originals.

2 Split the damaged shakes or shingles, using a hammer and chisel. Remove the pieces. Slide a hacksaw blade under the overlapping shingles and cut the nail heads. Pry out the remaining pieces of the shakes or shingles.

3 Gently pry up, but don't remove, the shakes or shingles above the repair area. Cut new pieces for the lowest course, leaving a ⅜" gap between pieces. Nail replacements in place with ring-shank siding nails. Fill in all but the top course in the repair area.

4 Cut the shakes or shingles for the top course. Because the top course can't be nailed, use roofing cement to fasten the pieces in place. Apply a coat of roofing cement where the shakes or shingles will sit, then slip them beneath the overlapping pieces. Press down to seat them in the roofing cement.

How to Patch Valley Flashing

TIP: *Use the same material for your patch as the original flashing. When dissimilar materials are joined, corrosion accelerates.*

1 Measure the damaged area and mark an outline for the patch. Cut a patch wide enough to fit under shingles on both sides of the repair area, and tapered to a point at one end. Using a trowel or flat pry bar, carefully break the seal between the damaged flashing and surrounding shingles.

2 Scrub the damaged flashing with a wire brush, and wipe it clean. Apply a heavy bead of roofing cement to the back of the patch. Cut a slit in the old flashing. Insert the tapered end of the patch into the slit, and slip the side edges under the shingles.

3 Rest the square end of the patch on top of the old flashing, and press it firmly to seal the roofing cement joint. Add roofing cement to the exposed seams. Using a trowel, feather out the cement to create a smooth path for water flow.

How to Replace Vent Flashing

Sleeve

1 Remove the shingles above and on the sides of the vent pipe. Remove the old vent flashing, using a flat pry bar. Apply a heavy, double bead of roofing cement along the bottom edge of the flange of the new flashing. Set the new flashing in place so it covers at least one course of shingles. Nail around the perimeter of the flange, using rubber-gasket nails.

2 Cut the shingles to fit around the neck of the flashing so they lie flat against the flange. Apply roofing cement to the shingle and flashing joints, and cover any exposed nail heads.

How to Replace Step Flashing

TIP: *When replacing flashing around masonry, such as a chimney, use copper or galvanized steel. Lime from mortar can corrode aluminum.*

1 Carefully bend up the counterflashing or the siding covering the damaged flashing. Cut any roofing cement seals, and pull back the shingles. Use a flat pry bar to remove the damaged flashing.

2 Cut the new flashing to fit, and apply roofing cement to all unexposed edges. Slip the flashing in place, making sure it's overlapped by the flashing above and overlaps the flashing and shingle below.

3 Drive one roofing nail through the flashing, at the bottom corner, and into the roof deck. Do not fasten the flashing to the vertical roof element, such as the chimney.

4 Reposition the shingles and counterflashing, and seal all joints with roofing cement.

Evaluating Siding & Trim

Check window and door trim for rot, especially on horizontal surfaces and at joints. Try to make repairs without removing the trim.

The first step in inspecting and evaluating siding and trim is to identify the type of material used on the house. Once you determine the material, take a close look at the problem area and determine the best method to fix it. If your siding is still under warranty, read through the warranty document before starting any repairs. Making repairs yourself could invalidate the product warranty. If the siding was professionally installed, you may want to talk to your contractor about the repairs.

In addition to looking unsightly, small siding problems can escalate into larger and more costly problems. As soon as you spot any siding damage, take steps to fix it immediately, especially if there's a possibility of water infiltration.

Tips for Inspecting Trim

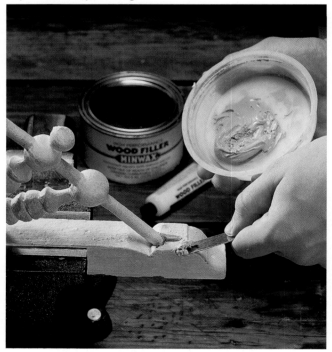

Inspect decorative trim, like the gingerbread trim shown here. If you suspect damage, remove the trim and make repairs in a workshop.

Evaluate broad trim pieces, such as the end cap trim shown above, and make repairs, using the same techniques as for siding.

Common Siding Problems

Separated joints can occur in any type of lap siding, but they're most common in wood lap. Gaps between ⅛" and ¼" thick can be filled with caulk. Gaps ⅜" or wider could mean that your house has a serious moisture or shifting problem. Consult a building inspector.

Buckling occurs most frequently in manufactured siding, when expansion gaps are too small at the points where the siding fits into trim and channels. If possible, move the channels slightly to give the siding more room. If not, remove the siding, trim the length slightly, then reinstall.

Minor surface damage to metal siding is best left alone in most cases—unless the damage has penetrated the surface. With metal products, cosmetic surface repairs often look worse than the damage.

Missing siding, such as cedar shakes that have been blown away from the wall, should be replaced immediately. Check the surrounding siding to make sure it's secure.

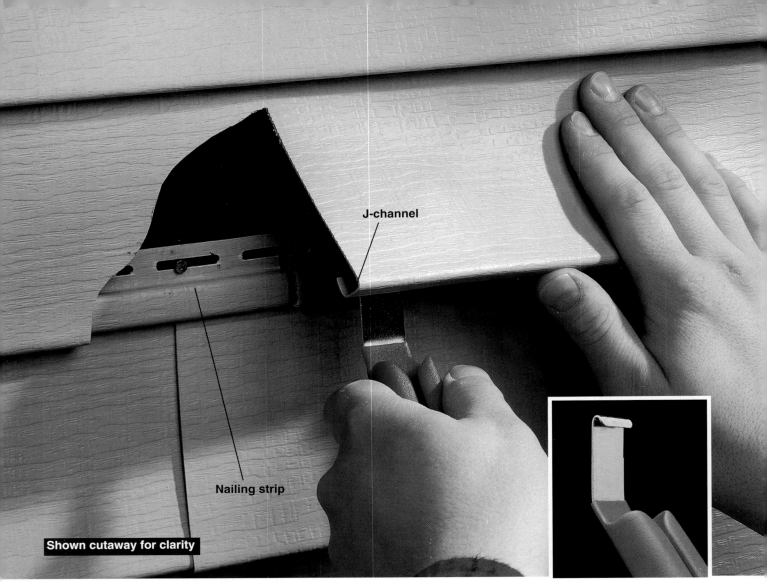

J-channel

Nailing strip

Shown cutaway for clarity

Vinyl and metal siding panels have a locking J-channel that fits over the bottom of the nailing strip on the underlying piece. Use a zip-lock tool (inset) to separate panels. Insert the tool at the seam nearest the repair area. Slide it over the J-channel, pulling outward slightly, to unlock the joint from the siding below.

Repairing Siding

Damage to siding is fairly common, but fortunately, it's also easy to fix. Small to medium holes, cracks, and rotted areas can be repaired with filler or by replacing the damaged sections with matching siding.

If you cannot find matching siding for repairs at building centers, check with salvage yards or siding contractors. When repairing aluminum or vinyl siding, contact the manufacturer or the contractor who installed the siding to help you locate matching materials and parts. If you're unable to find an exact match, remove a section of original siding from a less visible area of the house, such as the back of the garage, and use it for the patch. Cover the gap in the less visible

area with a close matching siding, where the mismatch will be less noticeable.

Everything You Need

Tools: aviation snips, caulk gun, drill, flat pry bar, hammer, straightedge, tape measure, utility knife, zip-lock tool, chisel, trowel, screwdrivers, hacksaw, circular saw, jig saw, key hole saw, flat pry bar, nail set, stud finder, paintbrush.

Materials: epoxy wood filler, epoxy glue, galvanized ring-shank siding nails, siliconized acrylic caulk, roofing cement, 30# felt paper, sheathing, trim, replacement siding, end caps, wood preservative, primer, paint or stain, metal sandpaper.

How to Repair Vinyl Siding

TIP: If the damaged panel is near a corner, door, or window, replace the entire panel. This eliminates an extra seam.

1 Starting at the seam nearest the damaged area, unlock interlocking joints, using a ziplock tool. Insert spacers between the panels, then remove the fasteners in the damaged siding, using a flat pry bar. Cut out the damaged area, using aviation snips. Cut a replacement piece 4" longer than the open area, and trim 2" off the nailing strip from each end. Slide the piece into position.

2 Insert siding nails in the nailing strip, then position the end of a flat pry bar over each nail head. Drive the nails by tapping on the neck of the pry bar with a hammer. Place a scrap piece of wood between the pry bar and siding to avoid damaging the siding. Slip the locking channel on the overlapping piece over the nailing strip of the replacement piece.

How to Patch Aluminum Siding

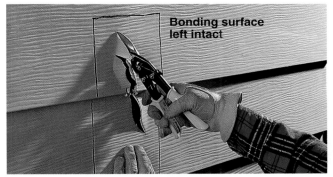

Bonding surface left intact

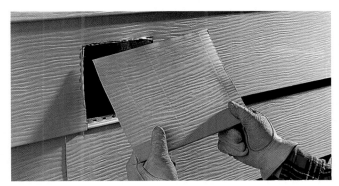

1 Cut out the damaged area, using aviation snips. Leave an exposed area on top of the uppermost piece to act as a bonding surface. Cut a patch 4" larger than the repair area. Remove the nailing strip. Smooth the edges with metal sandpaper.

2 Nail the lower patch in place by driving siding nails through the nailing flange. Apply roofing cement to the back of the top piece, then press it into place, slipping the locking channel over the nailing strip of the underlying piece. Caulk the seams.

How to Replace Aluminum End Caps

1 Remove the damaged end cap. If necessary, pry the bottom loose, then cut along the top with a hacksaw blade. Starting at the bottom, attach the replacement end caps by driving siding nails through the nailing tabs and into the framing members.

2 Trim the nailing tabs off the top replacement cap. Apply roofing cement to its back. Slide the cap over the locking channels of the siding panels. Press the top cap securely in place.

How to Replace Board & Batten Siding

1 Remove the battens over the damaged boards. Pry out the damaged boards in their entirety. Inspect the underlying house-wrap, and patch if necessary.

2 Cut replacement boards from the same type of lumber, allowing a ⅛" gap at the side seams. Prime or seal the edges and the back side of the replacement boards. Let them dry.

3 Nail the new boards in place, using ring-shank siding nails. Replace the battens and any other trim. Prime and paint or stain the new boards to blend with the surrounding siding.

How to Replace Wood Shakes & Shingles

1 Split damaged shakes or shingles with a hammer and chisel, and remove them. Insert wood spacers under the shakes or shingles above the repair area, then slip a hacksaw blade under the top board to cut off any remaining nail heads.

2 Cut replacement shakes or shingles to fit, leaving a ⅛"- to ¼"-wide gap at each side. Coat all sides and edges with wood preservative. Slip the patch pieces under the siding above the repair area. Drive siding nails near the top of the exposed area on the patches. Cover nail heads with caulk. Remove the spacers.

How to Replace Lap Siding

1 If the damage is caused by water, locate and repair the leak or other source of the water damage.

TIP: Use an electronic studfinder to locate framing members, or look for the nail heads.

2 Mark the area of siding that needs to be replaced. Make the cutout lines over the center of the framing members on each side of the repair area, staggering the cuts to offset the joints.

3 Insert spacers beneath the board above the repair area. Make entry cuts at the top of the cutting lines with a keyhole saw, then saw through the boards and remove them. Pry out any nails or cut off the nail heads, using a hacksaw blade. Patch or replace the sheathing and building paper, if necessary.

4 Measure and cut replacement boards to fit, leaving an expansion gap of ⅛" at each end. Use the old boards as templates to trace cutouts for fixtures and openings. Use a jig saw to make the cutouts. Apply wood sealer or primer to the ends and backs of the boards. Let them dry.

TIP: If you removed the bottom row of siding, nail a 1 × 2 starter strip along the bottom of the patch area.

5 Nail the new boards in place with siding nails, starting with the lowest board in the repair area. At each framing member, drive nails through the bottom of the new board and the top of the board below.

6 Fill expansion joints with caulk (use paintable caulk for painted wood or tinted caulk for stained wood). Prime and paint or stain the replacement boards to match the surrounding siding.

Repairing Masonry Walls

For walls with internal damaged areas, remove only the damaged section, keeping the upper layers intact if they are in good condition. Do not remove more than four adjacent bricks in one area—if the damaged area is larger, it will require temporary support, which is a job for a professional mason.

Masonry repairs are doomed to fail if the underlying causes of the problems aren't addressed. For example, masonry bricks can separate if the structure is still being subjected to the stress that caused the original damage.

Pinpoint the nature and cause of the problems before you start repairs. Look for obvious clues, such as overgrown tree roots or damaged gutters that let water drain onto masonry surfaces. Also check the slope of the surrounding landscape to see if it needs to be regraded to direct water away from the foundation. After you're sure you've eliminated the problem, you're ready to repair the damage.

Everything You Need

Tools: angle grinder with a masonry-cutting disc, mason's chisel, hammer, wire brush, pointing trowel, masonry trowel, jointing tool.

Materials: mortar mix, concrete fortifier, mortar pigment.

Types of Brick Problems

Deteriorating mortar joints are common and usually more widespread than surface deterioration of bricks. If you find damaged mortar, probe surrounding joints with a screwdriver to determine if they're sound. Tuckpoint deteriorating joints by removing cracked, damaged mortar, then filling the joints with fresh mortar.

Spalling occurs when trapped moisture is exposed to repeated freeze and thaw cycles, exerting enough directional pressure to fracture bricks. If the damage is contained to a fairly small area, you can replace only the affected bricks (opposite page). If the problem is more widespread, the structure may have to be replaced.

How to Replace Damaged Brick

1 Use an angle grinder with a masonry-cutting disc to score lines on the damaged brick and in the surrounding mortar joints.

2 Break the brick apart along the scored lines, using a masonry chisel and hammer. If removing several bricks, work from the top down, one row at a time. Be careful not to damage surrounding bricks.

TIP: *Save fragments from broken bricks to use as color references when shopping for replacement bricks.*

3 Chisel out any mortar remaining in the cavity, then brush away dirt and debris, using a wire brush. Rinse the area with water.

4 Mix the mortar, adding concrete fortifier and, if necessary, pigment to match the old mortar. Use a pointing trowel to apply a 1"-thick layer of mortar to the bottom and sides of the cavity.

5 Dampen the replacement brick slightly, then apply mortar to the ends and top. Fit the brick into the cavity and tap it with the handle of the trowel until the face is flush with the surrounding bricks. If needed, press more mortar into the joints, using a pointed trowel.

6 Scrape away excess mortar with a masonry trowel. Smooth the joints, using a jointing tool that matches the profile of the surrounding joints. Let the mortar set until crumbly, then brush away any excess.

Repairing Stucco Walls

Although stucco siding is very durable, it can be damaged, and over time it can crumble or crack. The directions given below work well for patching small areas less than two sq. ft. For more extensive damage, the repair is done in layers, as shown on the opposite page.

Everything You Need

Tools: caulk gun, disposable paintbrush, putty knife, mason's trowel, square-end trowel, hammer, whisk broom, wire brush, masonry chisel, aviation snips, pry bar, drill with masonry bit, scratching tool.

Materials: metal primer, stucco patching compound, bonding adhesive, denatured alcohol, metal primer, stucco mix, masonry paint, 1½" roofing nails, 15# building paper, self-furring metal lath, masonry caulk, tint, metal stop bead.

Fill thin cracks in stucco walls with masonry caulk. Overfill the crack with caulk, and feather until it's flush with the stucco. Allow the caulk to set, then paint it to match the stucco. Masonry caulk stays semiflexible, preventing further cracking.

How to Patch Small Areas

1 Remove loose material from the repair area, using a wire brush. Use the brush to clean away rust from any exposed metal lath, then apply a coat of metal primer to the lath.

2 Apply premixed stucco repair compound to the repair area, slightly overfilling the hole, using a putty knife or trowel. Read manufacturer's directions, as drying times vary.

3 Smooth the repair with a putty knife or trowel, feathering the edges to blend into the surrounding surface. Use a whisk broom or trowel to duplicate the original texture. Let the patch dry for several days, then touch it up with masonry paint.

How to Repair Large Areas

TIP: *Premixed stucco works well for small jobs, but for large ones, it's more economical to mix your own.*

1 Make a starter hole with a drill and masonry bit, then use a masonry chisel and hammer to chip away stucco in the repair area. Note: Wear safety glasses and a particle mask or respirator when cutting stucco. Cut self-furring metal lath to size and attach it to the sheathing, using roofing nails. Overlap pieces by 2". If the patch extends to the base of the wall, attach a metal stop bead at the bottom.

2 To mix your own stucco, combine three parts sand, two parts portland cement, and one part masonry cement. Add just enough water so the mixture holds its shape when squeezed (inset). Mix only as much as you can use in one hour.

3 Apply a ⅜"-thick layer of stucco directly to the metal lath. Push the stucco into the mesh until it fills the gap between the mesh and the sheathing. Score horizontal grooves into the wet surface, using a scratching tool. Let the stucco dry for two days, misting it with water every two to four hours.

4 Apply a second, smooth layer of stucco. Build up the stucco to within ¼" of the original surface. Let the patch dry for two days, misting every two to four hours.

5 Combine finish-coat stucco mix with just enough water for the mixture to hold its shape. Dampen the patch area, then apply the finish coat to match the original surface. Dampen the patch periodically for a week. Let it dry for several more days before painting.

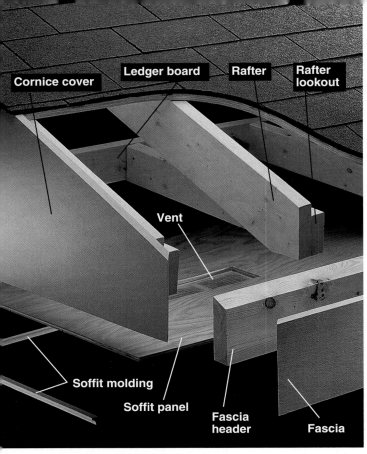

Cornice cover · **Ledger board** · **Rafter** · **Rafter lookout**

Vent

Soffit molding

Soffit panel · **Fascia header** · **Fascia**

Fascia and soffits close off the eaves area beneath the roof overhang. The fascia covers the ends of rafters and rafter lookouts, and provides a surface for attaching gutters. Soffits are protective panels that span the area between the fascia and the side of the house.

Repairing Wood Fascia & Soffits

Fascia and soffits add a finished look to your roof and promote a healthy roof system. A well-ventilated soffit system prevents moisture from building up under the roof and in the attic.

Most fascia and soffit problems can be corrected by cutting out sections of damaged material and replacing them. Joints between fascia boards are lock-nailed at rafter locations, so you should remove whole sections of fascia to make accurate bevel cuts for patches. Soffits can often be left in place for repairs.

Everything You Need

Tools: circular saw, jig saw, drill, putty knife, hammer, flat pry bar, nail set, chisel, caulk gun, paintbrush.

Materials: replacement materials, nailing strips, 2" and 2½" galvanized deck screws, 4d galvanized casing nails, acrylic caulk, primer, paint.

How to Repair Wood Fascia

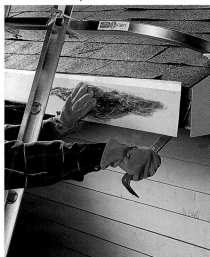

1 Remove gutters, shingle moldings, and any other items mounted on the fascia. Carefully pry off the damaged fascia board, using a pry bar. Remove the entire board and all old nails.

2 Set your circular saw for a 45° bevel, and cut off the damaged portion of the fascia board. Reattach the undamaged original fascia to the rafters or rafter lookouts, using 2" deck screws. Bevel-cut a patch board to replace the damaged section.

Rafter · **Old** · **New**

3 Set the patch board in place. Drill pilot holes through both fascia boards into the rafter. Drive nails in the holes to create a lock-nail joint (inset). Replace shingle moldings and trim pieces, using 4d casing nails. Set the nail heads. Prime and paint the new board.

How to Repair Wood Panel Soffits

TIP: *Cut soffits as close as possible to the rafters or rafter lookouts. Finish cuts with a chisel, if necessary.*

1 In the area where soffits are damaged, remove the support moldings that hold the soffits in place along the fascia and exterior wall. Drill entry holes, then use a jig saw to cut out the damaged soffit area.

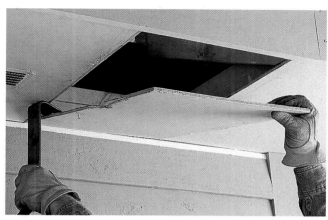

2 Remove the damaged soffit section, using a pry bar. Cut nailing strips the same length as the exposed area of the rafters, and fasten them to the rafters or rafter lookouts at the edges of the openings, using 2½" deck screws.

3 Using soffit material similar to the original panel, cut a replacement piece ⅛" smaller than the opening. If the new panel will be vented, cut the vent openings.

4 Attach the replacement panel to the nailing strips, using 2" deck screws. If you are not going to paint the entire soffit after the repair, prime and paint the replacement piece before installing it.

5 Reattach the soffit molding, using 4d casing nails. Set the nail heads.

6 Using siliconized acrylic caulk, fill all nail holes, screw holes, and gaps. Smooth out the caulk with a putty knife until the caulk is even with the surface. Prime and paint the soffit panels.

Repair delicate or ornamental trim molding in your workshop, whenever possible. You'll get better results than if you try repairing it while it's still attached.

Repairing Trim

Some exterior trim serves as decoration, like gingerbread and ornate cornice moldings. Other trim, such as brick molding and end caps, works with siding to seal your house from the elements. Damaged brick molding and corner boards should be patched with stock material similar to the original.

If you cannot find matching replacement parts for decorative trim at home improvement stores, check salvage shops or contact a custom millworker.

Everything You Need

Tools: hammer, chisel, circular saw, nail set, putty knife, utility knife, paintbrush, flat pry bar, caulk gun.

Materials: epoxy wood filler, epoxy glue, caulk, 10d galvanized casing nails, galvanized ring-shank siding nails, sandpaper, paint, building paper, drip edge, replacement trim.

Tips for Repairing & Replacing Trim

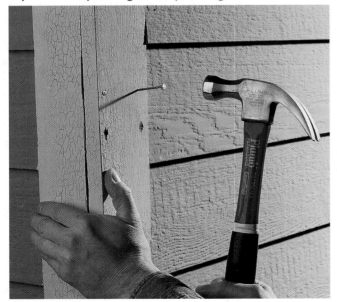

Reattach loose trim with new ring-shank siding nails driven near old nail locations. Fill old nail holes with paintable caulk, and touch up caulk and new nail heads with paint to match the surrounding surface.

Repair decorative trim molding with epoxy glue or wood filler. For major repairs, make your own replacement parts, or take the trim to a custom millwork shop.

How to Replace Brick Molding

1 Pry off old brick molding around windows and doors, using a flat pry bar. Remove any old drip edge. Inspect and repair the building paper.

2 Hold a replacement piece of brick molding, slightly longer than the original piece, across the opening. Mark cutting lines to fit the opening. Cut the replacement molding at the marks, matching any miter cuts.

3 Cut a 3"-wide piece of flashing to fit between the jambs, then bend it in half lengthwise to form the new drip edge (preformed drip edge is also available). Slip it between the siding and building paper, above the door or window. Do not nail the drip edge in place.

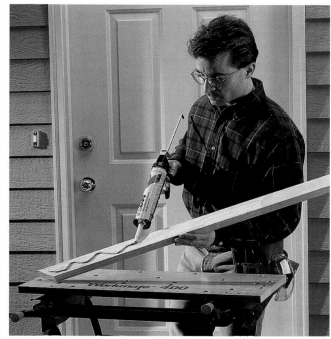

4 Test-fit the replacement piece of brick molding, then apply exterior-grade panel adhesive to the back side. Follow the manufacturer's directions for allowing the adhesive to set.

5 Nail the brick molding to the door header, using 10d galvanized casing nails. Lock-nail the miter joints, and set all nail heads. Seal joints, and cover nail holes with caulk. Prime and paint when the caulk dries.

Keep gutters and downspouts clean so rain falling on the roof is directed well away from the foundation. Nearly all wet basement problems are caused by water collecting near the foundation, a situation that can frequently be traced to clogged and overflowing gutters and downspouts.

Repairing Gutters

Gutters perform the important task of channeling water away from your house. A good gutter system prevents damage to your siding, foundation, and landscaping, and it helps prevent water from leaking into your basement. When gutters fail, evaluate the type and extent of damage to select the best repair method. Clean your gutters and downspouts as often as necessary to keep the system working efficiently.

Everything You Need

Tools: flat pry bar, hacksaw, caulk gun, pop rivet gun, drill, hammer, stiff-bristled brush, putty knife, steel wool, aviation snips, level, paintbrush, trowel, garden hose, chalk line.

Materials: Wood scraps, replacement gutter materials, siliconized acrylic caulk, roofing cement, metal flashing, sheet-metal screws or pop rivets, gutter hangers, primer and paint, gutter patching kit, gutter guards.

Use a trowel to clean leaves, twigs, and other debris out of the gutters before starting the repairs.

How to Unclog Gutters

1 Flush clogged downspouts with water. Wrap a large rag around a garden hose and insert it in the downspout opening. Arrange the rag so it fills the opening, then turn on the water full force.

2 Check the slope of the gutters, using a level. Gutters should slope slightly toward the downspouts. Adjust the hangers, if necessary.

3 Place gutter guards over the gutters to prevent future clogs.

How to Rehang Sagging Gutters & Patch Leaks

TIP: *A good slope for gutters is a ¼" drop every 10 ft. toward the downspouts.*

1 For sagging gutters, snap a chalk line on the fascia that follows the correct slope. Remove hangers in and near the sag. Lift the gutter until it's flush with the chalk line.

2 Reattach hangers every 24", and within 12" of seams. Use new hangers, if necessary. Avoid using the original nail holes. Fill small holes and seal minor leaks, using gutter caulk.

3 Use a gutter patching kit to make temporary repairs to a gutter with minor damage. Follow manufacturer's directions. For permanent repairs, see pages 246 to 247.

How to Repair Leaky Joints

1 Drill out the rivets or unfasten the metal screws to disassemble the leaky joint. Scrub both parts of the joint with a stiff-bristled brush. Clean the damaged area with water, and allow to dry completely.

2 Apply caulk to the joining parts, then reassemble the joint. Secure the connection with pop rivets or sheet-metal screws.

How to Patch Metal Gutters

TIP: To prevent corrosion, make sure the patch is the same type of metal as the gutter.

1 Clean the area around the damage with a stiff-bristled brush. Scrub it with steel wool or an abrasive pad to loosen residue, then rinse it with water.

2 Apply a ⅛"-thick layer of roofing cement evenly over the damage. Spread the roofing cement a few inches past the damaged area on all sides.

3 Cut and bend a piece of flashing to fit inside the gutter. Bed the patch in the roofing cement. Feather out the cement to reduce ridges so it won't cause significant damming.

How to Replace a Section of Metal Gutter

TIP: *If the damaged area is more than 2 ft. long, replace the entire section with new material.*

1 Remove gutter hangers in and near the damaged area. Insert wood spacers in the gutter, near each hanger, before prying.

2 Slip spacers between the gutter and fascia, near each end of the damaged area, so you won't damage the roof when cutting the gutter. Cut out the damaged section, using a hacksaw.

3 Cut a new gutter section at least 4" longer than the damaged section.

4 Clean the cut ends of the old gutter, using a wire brush. Caulk the ends, then center the gutter patch over the cutout area and press into the caulk.

5 Secure the gutter patch with pop rivets or sheet-metal screws. Use at least three fasteners at each joint. On the inside surfaces of the gutter, caulk over the heads of the fasteners.

6 Reinstall gutter hangers. If necessary, use new hangers, but don't use old holes. Prime and paint the patch to match the existing gutter.

Contributors

Alcoa Home Exteriors, Inc.
Omega Corporate Center
1590 Omega Drive
Pittsburgh, PA 15205
800-962-6973
www.alcoahomes.com

Alside
P.O. Box 2010
Akron, OH 44309
800-922-6009
www.alside.com

CertainTeed Corporation
750 E. Swedesford Road
Valley Forge, PA 19482
800-782-8777
www.certainteed.com

Dupont
4417 Lancaster Pike
Wilmington, DE 19805
800-44-TYVEK
www.tyvek.com

Easy Heat Inc.
31977 U.S. 20 East
New Carlisle, IN 46552
800-537-4732
www.easyheat.com

GAF Materials Corporation
1361 Alps Road
Wayne, NJ 07470
973-628-3000
www.gaf.com

James Hardie® Siding Products
26300 La Alameda
Mission Viejo, CA 92691
866-4-HARDIE
www.jameshardie.com

Mark Klindworth Siding
6140 Doffing Avenue
St. Paul, MN 55076
612-812-5146

La Habra Stucco
240 S. Loara Street
Anaheim, CA 92803
877-547-8822
www.lahabrastucco.com

M.C.A. Superior Clay Roof Tile
1985 Sampson Avenue
Corona, CA 92879
800-736-6221
www.mca-tile.com

MetalWorks
1005 Beaver Grade Road
Moon Township, PA 15108
800-320-0101
www.metalworksroof.com

Metal Sales Mfg. Corp.
7800 State Road 60
Sellersburg, IN 47172
800-406-7387
www.metalsales.us.com

Midwest Lumber
P.O. Box 800
Stillwater, MN 55082
800-862-6003
www.midwestlumberinc.com

O'Hagin's Inc.
2661 Gravenstein Hwy. South
Suite 107
Sebastopol, CA 95472
707-823-4762
www.ohaginvent.com

Owens Corning
One Owens Corning Pkwy.
Toledo, OH 43659
800-GET-PINK
www.owenscorning.com

Rocky Mountain Log Homes
1883 Hwy. 93 South
Hamilton, MT 59840
406-363-5680
www.rmlh.com

Roof Depot, Inc.
1860 East 28th Street
Minneapolis, MN 55407
800-458-8534
www.roofdepot.com

Vande Hey Raleigh
1665 Bohm Drive
Little Chute, WI 54140
920-766-0156
www.vrmtile.com

Vulcan Supply Corporation
P.O. Box 100
Westford, VT 05494
800-659-4732
www.vulcansupply.com

Resources

**National Roofing Contractors
Association (NRCA)**
10255 W. Higgins Road
Suite 600
Rosemont, IL 60018
847-299-9070
www.nrca.net

The Brick Industry Association
11490 Commerce Park Drive
Reston, VA 20191-1525
703-620-0010
www.bia.org

Metal Roofing Alliance
E. 4142 Hwy. 302
Belfair, WA 98528
360-275-6164
www.metalroofing.com

Roof Tile Institute
230 E. Ohio Street
Suite 400
Chicago, IL 60611-3265
888-321-9236
www.rooftile.org

Schmidt Roofing
138 W. 98th Street
Bloomington, MN 55420
952-888-4889

The Vinyl Siding Institute
1801 K Street N.W.
Suite 600K
Washington, DC 20006
888-367-8741
www.vinylsiding.org

**Western Red Cedar Lumber
Association**
P.O. Box 952
Riverhead, NY 11901-2136
604-684-0266
www.wrcla.org

**Western Wood Products
Association**
522 S.W. Fifth Avenue
Suite 500
Portland, OR 97204-2122
503-224-3930
www.wwpa.org

Photographers

Jessie Walker Associates
Glencoe, Il.
© Jessie Walker: pp. 13, 106, 134.
© Jessie Walker for Tom Swarthout:
p. 80.

Conversion Charts

Lumber Dimensions

Nominal - U.S.	Actual - U.S.	Metric		Nominal - U.S.	Actual - U.S.	Metric
1 × 2	¾" × 1½"	19 × 38 mm		1½ × 4	1¼" × 3½"	32 × 89 mm
1 × 3	¾" × 2½"	19 × 64 mm		1½ × 6	1¼" × 5½"	32 × 140 mm
1 × 4	¾" × 3½"	19 × 89 mm		1½ × 8	1¼" × 7¼"	32 × 184 mm
1 × 5	¾" × 4½"	19 × 114 mm		1½ × 10	1¼" × 9¼"	32 × 235 mm
1 × 6	¾" × 5½"	19 × 140 mm		1½ × 12	1¼" × 11¼"	32 × 286 mm
1 × 7	¾" × 6¼"	19 × 159 mm		2 × 4	1½" × 3½"	38 × 89 mm
1 × 8	¾" × 7¼"	19 × 184 mm		2 × 6	1½" × 5½"	38 × 140 mm
1 × 10	¾" × 9¼"	19 × 235 mm		2 × 8	1½" × 7¼"	38 × 184 mm
1 × 12	¾" × 11¼"	19 × 286 mm		2 × 10	1½" × 9¼"	38 × 235 mm
1¼ × 4	1" × 3½"	25 × 89 mm		2 × 12	1½" × 11¼"	38 × 286 mm
1¼ × 6	1" × 5½"	25 × 140 mm		3 × 6	2½" × 5½"	64 × 140 mm
1¼ × 8	1" × 7¼"	25 × 184 mm		4 × 4	3½" × 3½"	89 × 89 mm
1¼ × 10	1" × 9¼"	25 × 235 mm		4 × 6	3½" × 5½"	89 × 140 mm
1¼ × 12	1" × 11¼"	25 × 286 mm				

Metric Conversions

To Convert:	To:	Multiply by:		To Convert:	To:	Multiply by:
Inches	Millimeters	25.4		Millimeters	Inches	0.039
Inches	Centimeters	2.54		Centimeters	Inches	0.394
Feet	Meters	0.305		Meters	Feet	3.28
Yards	Meters	0.914		Meters	Yards	1.09
Square inches	Square centimeters	6.45		Square centimeters	Square inches	0.155
Square feet	Square meters	0.093		Square meters	Square feet	10.8
Square yards	Square meters	0.836		Square meters	Square yards	1.2
Ounces	Milliliters	30.0		Milliliters	Ounces	.033
Pints (U.S.)	Liters	0.473 (Imp. 0.568)		Liters	Pints (U.S.)	2.114 (Imp. 1.76)
Quarts (U.S.)	Liters	0.946 (Imp. 1.136)		Liters	Quarts (U.S.)	1.057 (Imp. 0.88)
Gallons (U.S.)	Liters	3.785 (Imp. 4.546)		Liters	Gallons (U.S.)	0.264 (Imp. 0.22)
Ounces	Grams	28.4		Grams	Ounces	0.035
Pounds	Kilograms	0.454		Kilograms	Pounds	2.2

Counterbore, Shank & Pilot Hole Diameters

Screw Size	Counterbore Diameter for Screw Head	Clearance Hole for Screw Shank	Pilot Hole Diameter	
			Hard Wood	Soft Wood
#1	.146 (9/64)	5/64	3/64	1/32
#2	1/4	3/32	3/64	1/32
#3	1/4	7/64	1/16	3/64
#4	1/4	1/8	1/16	3/64
#5	1/4	1/8	5/64	1/16
#6	5/16	9/64	3/32	5/64
#7	5/16	5/32	3/32	5/64
#8	3/8	11/64	1/8	3/32
#9	3/8	11/64	1/8	3/32
#10	3/8	3/16	1/8	7/64
#11	1/2	3/16	5/32	9/64
#12	1/2	7/32	9/64	1/8

Adhesives

Type	Characteristics	Uses
White glue	**Strength:** moderate; rigid bond **Drying time:** several hours **Resistance to heat:** poor **Resistance to moisture:** poor **Hazards:** none **Cleanup/solvent:** soap and water	**Porous surfaces:** Wood (indoors) Paper Cloth
Yellow glue (carpenter's glue)	**Strength:** moderate to good; rigid bond **Drying time:** several hours; faster than white glue **Resistance to heat:** moderate **Resistance to moisture:** moderate **Hazards:** none **Cleanup/solvent:** soap and water	**Porous surfaces:** Wood (indoors) Paper Cloth
Two-part epoxy	**Strength:** excellent; strongest of all adhesives **Drying time:** varies, depending on manufacturer **Resistance to heat:** excellent **Resistance to moisture:** excellent **Hazards:** fumes are toxic and flammable **Cleanup/solvent:** acetone will dissolve some types	**Smooth & porous surfaces:** Wood (indoors & outdoors) Metal Masonry Glass Fiberglass
Hot glue	**Strength:** depends on type **Drying time:** less than 60 seconds **Resistance to heat:** fair **Resistance to moisture:** good **Hazards:** hot glue can cause burns **Cleanup/solvent:** heat will loosen bond	**Smooth & porous surfaces:** Glass Plastics Wood
Cyanoacrylate (instant glue)	**Strength:** excellent, but with little flexibility **Drying time:** a few seconds **Resistance to heat:** excellent **Resistance to moisture:** excellent **Hazards:** can bond skin instantly; toxic, flammable **Cleanup/solvent:** acetone	**Smooth surfaces:** Glass Ceramics Plastics Metal
Construction adhesive	**Strength:** good to excellent; very durable **Drying time:** 24 hours **Resistance to heat:** good **Resistance to moisture:** excellent **Hazards:** may irritate skin and eyes **Cleanup/solvent:** soap and water (while still wet)	**Porous surfaces:** Framing lumber Plywood and paneling Wallboard Foam panels Masonry
Water-base contact cement	**Strength:** good **Drying time:** bonds instantly; dries fully in 30 minutes **Resistance to heat:** excellent **Resistance to moisture:** good **Hazards:** may irritate skin and eyes **Cleanup/solvent:** soap and water (while still wet)	**Porous surfaces:** Plastic laminates Plywood Flooring Cloth
Silicone sealant (caulk)	**Strength:** fair to good; very flexible bond **Drying time:** 24 hours **Resistance to heat:** good **Resistance to moisture:** excellent **Hazards:** may irritate skin and eyes **Cleanup/solvent:** acetone	**Smooth & porous surfaces:** Wood Ceramics Fiberglass Plastics Glass

Converting Temperatures

Convert degrees Fahrenheit (F) to degrees Celsius (C) by following this simple formula: Subtract 32 from the Fahrenheit temperature reading. Then, mulitply that number by ⅝. For example, 77°F - 32 = 45. 45 × ⅝ = 25°C.

To convert degrees Celsius to degrees Fahrenheit, multiply the Celsius temperature reading by ⅝. Then, add 32. For example, 25°C × ⅝ = 45. 45 + 32 = 77°F.

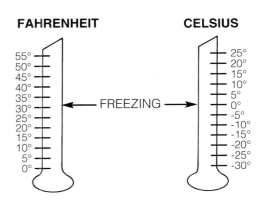

Index

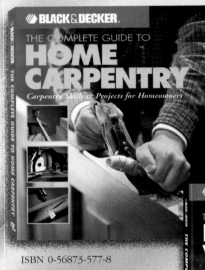
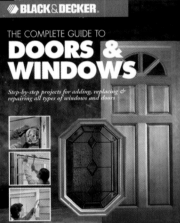
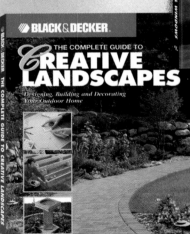